1997

SUTTON POCKET HISTORIES

THE
NORMAN
CONQUEST

N.J. HIGHAM

SUTTON PUBLISHING

First published in the United Kingdom in 1998 by
Sutton Publishing Limited · Phoenix Mill
Thrupp · Stroud · Gloucestershire · GL5 2BU

British Library Cataloguing in Publication Data
A catalogue record for this book is available from the British
Library.

ISBN 0-7509-1953-1

*Cover picture: A Battle Scene in an illuminated 'E' from a book of
Maccabees in the Library of Durham Cathedral (courtesy of the Dean
and Chapter of Durham Cathedral)*

ALAN SUTTON™ and SUTTON™ are the
trade marks of Sutton Publishing Limited

Typeset in 11/14.5 pt Baskerville.
Typesetting and origination by
Sutton Publishing Limited.
Printed in Great Britain by
The Guernsey Press Company Limited,
Guernsey, Channel Islands.

Contents

For my family and friends

List of Dates

1047	William obtains effective control over Normandy.
1051–2	Temporary exile of Godwine and his family from England.
1057	Return of Edward the Exile and Edgar the Atheling; death of Edward the Exile.
1065	Northumbrian rebellion and exile of Tostig.
1066	Death of Edward the Confessor; succession of Harold II (Godwineson); battles of Gate Fulford, Stamford Bridge and Hastings; coronation of William I.
1068	Exeter revolt; Edgar and Maerleswein flee to Scotland; revolt of Edwin, Morcar and the Northumbrians.
1069	Killing of Robert de Commines at Durham; Northumbrian rebellion and arrival of Danish fleet.
1069–70	William's devastation of the north.
1075	Revolt of the earls.
1085–6	Crisis of anticipated Danish invasion; Domesday Inquest and oath-taking ceremony at Salisbury.
1087	William's invasion of Vexin and his death; succession of Duke Robert to Normandy and William Rufus to England.
1096	Duke Robert departs on crusade, leaving William in control of Normandy.
1100	William Rufus killed in the New Forest; succeeded by his brother, Henry I; Henry marries Maud, niece of Edgar the Atheling; return of Duke Robert to Normandy.
1106	Henry I defeats and captures Duke Robert and reunites Normandy with England.

1135 Death of Henry I; succeeded in England and
   Normandy by his nephew, Stephen of Blois.

1141–4 Angevin conquest of Normandy on behalf of Matilda.

1154 Death of King Stephen; succeeded in England and
   Normandy by Henry II, Matilda's son, Count of Anjou
   and Maine and husband of Eleanor, Duchess of
   Aquitaine.

1202–4 King John's loss of Normandy.

SIMPLIFIED FAMILY TREE OF THE KINGS OF ENGLAND

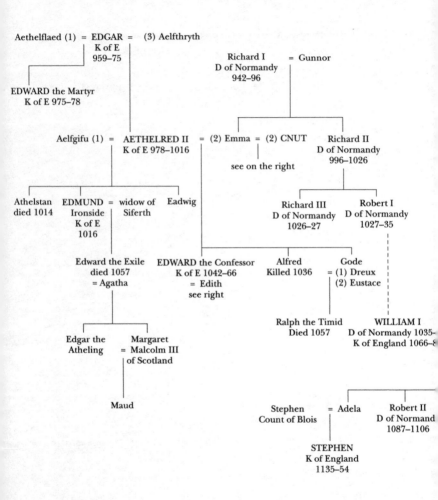

Aethelflaed (1) = EDGAR = (3) Aelfthryth
                   K of E
                   959–75

EDWARD the Martyr
K of E 975–78

Richard I
D of Normandy   = Gunnor
942–96

Aelfgifu (1) = AETHELRED II = (2) Emma = (2) CNUT   Richard II
               K of E 978–1016   D of Normandy
                                                      996–1026
                            see on the right

Athelstan   EDMUND = widow of   Eadwig   Richard III   Robert I
died 1014   Ironside Siferth   D of Normandy   D of Normandy
            K of E   1026–27   1027–35
            1016

      Edward the Exile   EDWARD the Confessor   Alfred   Gode
      died 1057   K of E 1042–66   Killed 1036   = (1) Dreux
      = Agatha   = Edith   (2) Eustace
                          see right

                                                Ralph the Timid   WILLIAM I
                                                Died 1057   D of Normandy 1035–
                                                                     K of England 1066–8

Edgar the   Margaret
Atheling   = Malcolm III
             of Scotland

      Maud
                                          Stephen   = Adela   Robert II
                                          Count of Blois   D of Normand
                                                                   1087–1106

                                                STEPHEN
                                                K of England
                                                1135–54

Capital Letters = Kings of England

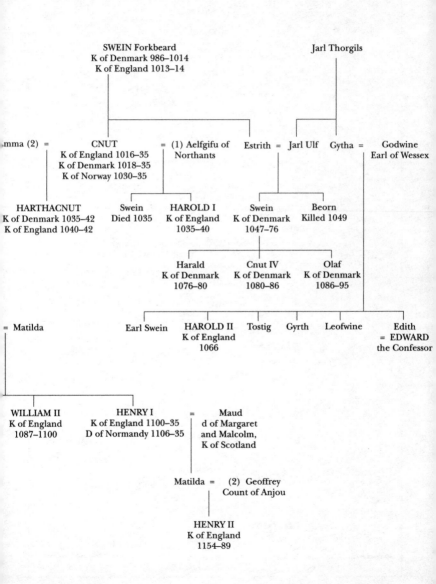

England and Normandy.

ONE

An Improbable King

'and William conquered this land'

Duke William of Normandy was crowned king at Westminster Abbey on Monday 25 December 1066. Before anointing him, Archbishop Ealdred of York required the duke to swear on the altar that he would 'defend the holy churches of God and their ministers, and would also rule justly and with royal care the people who were placed under him'. Outside, Norman soldiers took alarm at the English acclamation of the new king and, believing that a riot had started, began to fire the nearest suburbs. If these events do nothing else, they at least highlight the atmosphere of misunderstanding and distrust in which the reign of England's first Norman king commenced.

There was good cause for such distrust. William had begun the year as a rank outsider in the race for the crown, without any identifiable support inside England. His famed illegitimacy and his foreignness both counted against him and neither his careful wooing of support at Rome nor his hiring of French mercenaries can hide the weakness of his case. William's apologists made much of his position as the 'designated heir of the saintly Edward', but were unable to agree precisely how or when he had achieved that status. The longest and most elegiac account, that of William of Poitiers, made no effort to establish a chronology and it is left to the briefer comments of William of Jumièges to claim that Archbishop Robert was Edward's messenger back in 1051–2. The Worcester manuscript of the *Anglo-Saxon Chronicle* notes that William visited England at this date; if this is correct, it may have been connected. Yet whether or not William was Edward's officially nominated heir, a decade and a half would pass before the old king's death, and the political circumstances were very different.

Nor was William a descendant of the English royal family. Despite repeated statements regarding close kinship between them by his apologists, William's only blood connection with Edward was by virtue of his great-aunt Emma, Edward's mother, who had departed Normandy for Aethelred's court sixty-four years before 1066. Although Edward's long exile in Normandy may well have strengthened his Norman connections, it does little to reinforce William's candidacy.

All commentators were agreed that Edward's designation was crucial to his successor. Almost all were likewise at one in acknowledging Edward's support on his deathbed for Harold Godwineson, his principal lieutenant, premier earl and brother-in-law. In stark contrast to William, Harold had overwhelming support within the English political elite, almost all of whom rallied round his leadership unreservedly during the ten months that separated the death of Edward the Confessor from his own.

Even with Harold and his brothers slain at the battle of Hastings, William was still not the preferred candidate of the English. Edward the Confessor was desperately short of close kin but during the 1050s his council had arranged for the return of his half-nephew, Edward the Exile, from eastern Europe. This long-lost prince was presumably brought back as a prospective successor but unfortunately died on arrival. His son Edgar did, however, survive, and it was around this juvenile scion of the house of Cerdic that the English magnates rallied in the autumn of 1066. Even William's Norman apologists recognized the superiority of his claim by descent, while setting it aside in favour of their own patron.

How then did William justify his acquisition of the English throne? His apologists advanced a host of arguments centred on his worthiness by virtue of superior wisdom, great valour and prudence. Such qualities were explicitly his as gifts from God, and William of Poitiers in particular made much of this characterization of William as God's champion fighting for His justice. Duke William was portrayed as a figure whom not even the greatest warriors of the classical past could overshadow, and William of Poitiers made reference to such heroes as Agamemnon, Xerxes, Aeneas, Caesar, Marius and Pompey to make the point. His audience was left with an image of William the wise, the just and the strong, the rightness of whose candidacy God triumphantly upheld. This is the 'great man' theory of history with a vengeance.

William's cause was reinforced by the demolition of Harold's character. Harold was depicted as a notorious oath-breaker, his elevation as partisan and his coronation flawed by association with Archbishop Stigand, who was the object of anathema by three Popes. Harold was, moreover, unwilling to face William in single combat, and so was held personally responsible for the many deaths at Hastings.

Nor did the English in general escape censure. It was William of Jumièges' opinion that 'Christ recompensed them for the foul and unjust murder of Alfred, brother of King Edward', who had been killed in 1036. English opinion was less specific as to the cause but in agreement that the outcome reflected God's anger at themselves. One English chronicler lamented that 'the French remained masters of the field, even as God granted it to them because of the sins of the people'.

Yet, despite all their rhetoric, even William's staunchest apologists were in two minds as to what precisely had occurred and just how the duke best fitted into events. William was described by William of Jumièges at the same time both as the hereditary lord of the English and as 'their noble conqueror'. English reactions to his elevation varied enormously but a regular scattering of insurrections implies widespread resentment and a willingness to take considerable risks to defy him. Such revolts were generally poorly managed affairs but they occurred in each and every area of England and several posed a serious threat to the new regime. In consequence, William kept many of his English opponents in custody throughout his life but, conscious perhaps of his own salvation, thought to free the survivors on his deathbed. These included one of King Harold's sons, his brother and Earl Morcar.

Nor were William's French allies necessarily much in favour of his kingship. Count Eustace of Boulogne seems to have considered his own rights as Edward's brother-in-law equal to William's and attempted to take over in Kent during William's absence in 1067.

William's successors do not seem to have felt entirely confident of the legitimacy of their inheritance. Edgar Atheling found an ally in the Conqueror's eldest son, Duke Robert, and may have hoped to be reinstated to his ancestral throne should his patron succeed in the struggle for his father's inheritance. Robert's departure for the Holy Land interrupted this contest but his return in 1099 coincided with the murder of William Rufus, king of England, and the stage was set for Robert's final the Domesday Inquest of 1086. Furthermore, the twelfth century witnessed an enormous upsurge in interest in pre-Conquest precedent and evidences, of cults and land grants, for example, even to the point where many of the latter were forged. It witnessed in addition a great enthusiasm for English history. Eadmer at Canterbury eulogized the lives of King Edgar and St Dunstan as a veritable golden age, from which the present had fallen away. John of Worcester had the temerity to praise King Harold II, whom he represented as a 'great and true king', while Orderic Vitalis promoted many of his manly qualities. The great Anglo-Norman writer William of Malmesbury was fulsome in praise of the West Saxon dynasty (but less so of Harold) and critical of the general exclusion of Englishmen from high office in his own day. These and other twelfth-century writers recorded their pride in Englishness and love for the land itself, and we owe much of our knowledge of late Anglo-Saxon England to them. Many, including Orderic, were openly critical of William I's treatment of his new people. Such authors were responsible for the development of the story of Hereward the Wake, for example, the rebel and outlaw who was reinvented during the early twelfth century as a folk hero.

The very different treatment of the principal characters by near-contemporaries provided fertile ground for much later political thinkers and practitioners. The process began afresh in Elizabeth's reign, when the new Anglicanism sought to identify its roots in a pure Old English Church prior to its corruption by Norman (thus French and Catholic) influences. Thereafter, the 'Norman Yoke' was considered a suitable synonym for the Stuart monarchy by its opponents. From such beginnings, Anglo-Saxon England was naturally lauded by the great Whig historians, many of whom sought the origins of the distinctive English constitution and freedoms in pre-Conquest England, and interpretation of the Norman Conquest became imbued with English nationalism and imperialism, and regarded as a blow to the development of the constitution. The process found its most committed proponents in the second half of the nineteenth century: despite his huge admiration for the Normans, Lord Macaulay interpreted the Conquest as an awful tyranny, the curse of which was undone only by King John's losses in France and by the Magna Carta; E.A. Freeman and Lord Lytton carried such views to the extreme in their reinterpretation while G.O. Sayle rejected the 'Victorian illusion of progress' but still opposed the vision of cataclysmic change for the better which had tended to replace it. More recently detailed historical research on both sides of the Channel has brought recognition that Norman and English – and Normandy and England – were less different than had been supposed, and that the Conquest was less a matter of cultural and political imperialism and more one of synthesis. The published works of Ann Williams perhaps best exemplify the more balanced scholarship of the present generation.

Notwithstanding, the Conquest remains a cusp event in the history of England and William himself still presided over the twenty-year period which established Norman kingship. Whether he should be considered the great man of his own estimation (and David Douglas's reconstruction) or the 'lucky bastard' of John Gillingham's more caustic views, the decisiveness of his victory at Hastings seems beyond reasonable challenge. In a host of ways, the Norman Conquest and William himself still matter.

TWO

England, the Vikings and the Normans

In 1066 England was invaded by two great armies, Harald Hardrada's Scandinavian one and William's. Interactions between England, Scandinavia and Normandy were, however, nothing new: they were a critical feature of English history sixty years earlier in the reign of Aethelred; even earlier Edward the Elder (899–924) and Athelstan (924–39) were constructing marital alliances across western Europe, at the very time that Rollo, his son William Longsword and their Norsemen ('Normans') were establishing themselves in France.

In Aethelred's reign (978–1016) Viking raids on England resumed after two generations of peace. Several factors seem to have played their part: the regicide of Edward the Martyr brought the boy-king Aethelred to the throne and promised weak leadership combined with a deeply divided elite; the dynasty was long without adult heirs; improved equipment and increasing professionalism among the Vikings and rising resistance to their efforts from continental states such as the Saxon Empire – all may have contributed.

The first raids occurred just two years into the reign, targeting Cheshire, Southampton and Thanet. Such hit-and-run attacks thereafter gave way to more substantial fleets commanded by notable leaders such as Olaf Tryggvason, which targeted major settlement sites or extorted English silver as the price of peace. The assault was redoubled once King Swein of Denmark had established overall leadership of Scandinavia and was free to throw his considerable resources into raiding.

England was in many respects a well-defended state, with a network of walled towns (known as *burhs*), a fleet and both regional and central systems of raising armies. Ealdorman and, later, earls provided local foci of government and justice, and their retinues were the core of shire levies of armed men. Consequently England's inhabitants probably expected to see off their attackers. In 991, however, Vikings defeated and killed Byrhtnoth, the elderly but distinguished ealdorman of Essex – an event which was immortalized in the fine epic poem, *The Battle of Maldon*. The government paid off its assailants, and Danegeld was to become a commonplace but increasingly expensive means of combating Viking disruption over the years to come.

Aethelred's regime adopted several strategies by which to counter Viking attacks. One was diplomacy designed to secure allies or divide the opposition. Negotiations with Olaf Tryggvason led to his baptism and he departed enriched from England to establish himself as king in Norway in defiance of Swein. Papal diplomacy brokered a peace agreement between Aethelred and Duke Richard of Normandy in 991 but the latter died in 996 and his son, Richard II, seems to have harboured the Danish fleet in 1000. Aethelred sought the friendship of King Robert the Pious of France (996–1031) but Robert had no influence over the coastal areas. Thereafter, Richard II and Aethelred came to terms which they cemented by the marriage of Richard's youngest sister, Emma, to Aethelred in 1002.

Aethelred already had a large family by his first wife, Aelfgifu, but he seems to have laid great store by his new alliance. Emma was provided with extensive dower lands, including Exeter, and the marriage seems to have given Aethelred the confidence to launch the St Brice's Day massacre of Scandinavians in England that autumn. However, it did not deter Viking fleets penetrating the Channel to strike at England. Aethelred's behaviour as king changed soon after Emma bore Prince Edward (the Confessor) in about 1005 and it seems likely that he intended Emma's son, rather than his sons by Aelfgifu, to succeed him. The makeup of the ruling clique changed dramatically in 1006, with Aethelred's connivance in the murder of Ealdorman Aelfhelm and the blinding of his sons, and the rise of Eadric Streona.

Aethelred bought off the Danes and inaugurated a massive shipbuilding initiative ready for the campaigning season of 1009 but their mobilization at Sandwich ended in fiasco and faction, leaving England open to devastation by forces under Thorkell the Tall, who had to be bought off in April 1012. Thereafter, Aethelred took Thorkell into his own service. With Danish soldiery at their back, Aethelred and Eadric had arguably weathered the storm of Viking assault and stabilized the regime. However, the political community was by this date deeply divided: the men of Cambridgeshire had stubbornly withstood the Danes at Ringmere in 1010 and had suffered prominent casualties and savage raiding in consequence; Aethelred and Eadric's atrocities in 1006 had alienated powerful men in Lindsey and the 'Five Boroughs' and his elder sons had every reason to oppose attempts to divert the succession from themselves in favour of Aethelred's half-Norman offspring.

Aethelred's eldest son, Athelstan, seems to have been the focus of internal opposition to the court but he may already have been ill by 1012. He died, apparently from natural causes, in 1014. English critics reacted to Aethelred's engagement of Thorkell by allying with King Swein of Denmark. When Swein arrived in 1013 he sailed into the Trent as far as Gainsborough and was joined by the men of Northumbria, Lindsey, the 'Five Boroughs' and 'all the raiding army east of Watling Street', who acknowledged him as king without a blow being struck.

Against such an alliance, Aethelred was powerless and his forces could only hold London as Swein invaded southern England and negotiated the surrender of the West Saxons. By Christmas 1013 every English province had recognized Swein as king and given hostages, yet without a battle being fought. This speaks volumes for the unpopularity of Aethelred's regime and policies after 1006 and the king was forced to retire with his ships and his family by Emma to the Norman court.

Swein's kingship of England was, therefore, more a consequence of disillusion with Aethelred than an outright conquest. His son Cnut's marriage to Ealdorman Aelfhelm's daughter, Aelfgifu, identifies one at least of the principal foci of that disillusionment, and effectively constituted a marriage alliance. Their triumph was swept away, however, by Swein's sudden death in February 1014. The Danish fleet and men of Lindsey supported Cnut, but others of the English nobility extricated themselves, recalled and restored Aethelred and 'outlawed every Danish king from England forever'. They then expelled the Danes, ravaged Lindsey and allowed Aethelred and Eadric, at a great assembly at Oxford in 1015, to dispossess and murder Aelfhelm's kin.

Aethelred had relied heavily on both his Viking mercenaries and his Norman in-laws during this crisis. He now sought to destabilize Swein's successors by funding one of them, Olaf Haraldsson (St Olaf), in a bid for the throne of Norway. The English succession was, however, the critical issue. The old king was incapacitated by illness in 1015.

His eldest surviving son, Edmund Ironside, did not have his father's support so set about constructing his own power base as leader of the men of Lindsey and the 'Five Boroughs'. Cnut returned to England and secured the aid of Aethelred's favourite and son-in-law, Eadric Streona, who brought in the West Saxons. Another royal son-in-law, Earl Uhtred of Northumbria, backed Edmund. The contest was, therefore, not just between English and Danish armies but also between different sectors of the English elite and royal family, and had all the messiness characteristic of a dynastic civil war.

Aethelred eventually died at London on 23 April 1016, leaving Cnut and Edmund to fight for the throne. Despite his greater successes, Edmund's cause was wrecked by Eadric's manoeuvring and his consequent defeat at Ashingdon on 18 October. He held on to Wessex in the subsequent peace accord but died, probably of wounds received in battle, on 30 November.

Cnut sought to legitimize his reign by several strategies. Like Aethelred, he held a great assembly at Oxford and there he committed his regime to 'the laws of King Edgar', Aethelred's father. Thereafter, although his earlier marriage to Aelfgifu continued, he married Aethelred's widow, Emma, despite a sizeable age difference, and thus laid claim to membership of sorts of the English royal family. However, his early reign was fragile in the extreme and he did not pay off any of his forces until 1018, at the cost of a great geld. Potential opposition centred, of course, on Aethelred's surviving sons. Only Eadwig was of an age to resist and this he apparently did with West Saxon support in 1017. The plan was detected and several senior figures – including Eadric Streona – were liquidated. A second conspiracy in 1020 was similarly suppressed by Cnut and nothing more is known of Eadwig bar his burial at Tavistock, although later writers considered him innocent and held Cnut responsible for his death. Aethelred had only two grandsons, Edmund's sons Edward and Edmund, but they were infants during this crisis and were taken – or perhaps sent by Cnut – out of England, eventually to Hungary where Edward survived, married well and raised three children, including Edgar the Atheling.

Aethelred's remaining sons were Edward and Alfred, both born to Emma. Edward was probably born in 1005, Alfred not much before 1013. Both found refuge at the court of Emma's brothers

highlighted by, for example, Robin Fleming, but external appointees as earls gradually receded, with Godwine and Leofric becoming established as English *nouveaux riches* rulers of vast earldoms in Wessex and Mercia respectively. A century earlier, earldoms had rarely exceeded a single shire. For the rest of the Anglo-Saxon period, large earldoms which were almost sub-kingships were to be the norm.

Early on, Cnut proved exceptionally fortunate. His brother's early death enabled him to secure Denmark in 1020 and from this dual power base he attempted to control the entire Scandinavian world, reviving the pan-Viking hegemonies of his father and grandfather. However, resistance in the north proved stubborn. Although St Olaf was evicted from Norway in 1028 and killed in 1030, his son, Magnus, had successfully defeated Cnut's deputies by 1035. Cnut's episodic domination of Scandinavia and control of England made him the most formidable power in Europe west of Saxony and helps explain the amity which he enjoyed with Flanders and other parts of the continent. Cnut famously attended Conrad's imperial coronation at Rome in 1027 and his daughter Gunnhild was betrothed to the latter's son Henry in 1035. Even so, Cnut's rule of so many disparate kingdoms with so many different enemies required enormous energy as well as good fortune and his position was probably not tenable in the long term.

Cnut died on 12 November 1035 and was buried at Winchester. Norway had already been lost and his son Swein evicted (to die within the year). Harthacnut was king in Denmark and was probably his father's intended heir overall, but Norwegian hostility kept him in Scandinavia. In England, Harthacnut's absence gave his half-brother Harold an opportunity to press for the regency and ultimately the kingship, which he secured with the aid of the northern earls. Queen Emma called in Edward and Alfred to oppose Harold but Alfred was taken by Earl Godwine and died from brutal treatment. Edward returned to Normandy having found no English support when he sailed into Southampton. Duke Robert's death on pilgrimage to Jerusalem in 1035 robbed the athelings of much-needed support but their welcome was in any case uncertain. Cnut's regime had had two decades to consolidate its power. Many had profited from the consequent re-ordering of status and property and had reason to resist the pretensions of Aethelred's sons, despite their descent from Cerdic, and most looked to Cnut's sons to succeed their father.

THREE

Edward the Confessor

With Harold I on the English throne, Edward's
prospects were bleak. His intervention after Cnut's
death had failed ignominiously: his brother Alfred
was killed and his mother Emma was driven into
exile. Normandy had an illegitimate infant duke,
William, and was incapable of sponsoring further
expeditions. The only plausible challenge to Harold
was that posed by Harthacnut, but war with Norway
kept him in Denmark until 1040. Then his belated
journey south was met by English councillors in
Flanders with the news that his half-brother was
already dead. Harthacnut's presence was, however,
needed back in Denmark for the war with Norway.
He was barely known in England, unmarried and
had no obvious associate to guard his interests. It
may have been this that persuaded Harthacnut to
invite Edward, his elder half-brother, to England as
'king'. When Harthacnut in turn died prematurely

on 8 June 1042, Edward was well positioned to succeed.

Even so, it seems unlikely that there was much enthusiasm for his candidacy among an elite which owed its power and wealth to Cnut and his sons. Edward's descent from Aethelred posed dangers from their perspective and he took the throne largely by virtue of his kinship with Harthacnut. Having left in 1016, he was a stranger in England in 1042. He was middle aged, about thirty-seven, and lacked committed supporters. Queen Emma had only lately returned to England. Both Earl Leofric of Mercia and Earl Siward of Northumbria had backed Harold I. Earl Godwine's betrayal of Prince Alfred necessarily clouded relations with Edward. The leading churchmen were largely appointees of Cnut or Harold. Edward was, however, the only available candidate and his accession became an exercise in *real politique.* He did not have the external power that had underpinned previous regimes so had to accommodate existing power brokers. All the earls retained their established areas of influence and Edward additionally married Godwine's daughter Edith in 1045 and promoted Godwine's elder sons, Swein and Harold, to earldoms.

Edward negotiated the early years of his reign with considerable caution. A very few figures – such as Cnut's niece Gunnhild and the courtier Osgod Clapa – were expelled. At home, Godwine was allowed to expand the influence of his family into East Anglia and the Welsh marches, where it necessarily challenged Leofric. Edward's nephew, Ralph, was also promoted to an earldom in this region. Siward was permitted to consolidate his hold on Northumbria, where he had lately defeated the native House of Bamburgh, but Godwine obtained most from the early years of the reign.

Abroad, Edward's regime initially retained good relations with Flanders and Denmark, where Edward had a common interest with Cnut's nephew, Swein, in resisting Magnus (died 1047) and then Harald Hardrada of Norway. Anticipation of Norwegian attack led to Edward's mobilization in 1044 and 1045, and he and the earls pursued Viking raiders in 1048, but they refused to send aid to Swein in Denmark.

Edward himself arguably preferred the company of Normans and Frenchmen. Small numbers joined him from Normandy, including his nephew, and Edward directed some patronage in their direction.

The king employed continental priests in his household and promoted several Lotharingians and Normans to bishoprics, but this was balanced by the advancement of Englishmen such as Stigand, Queen Emma's favourite, to the dioceses of Elmham and then Winchester (1047). Despite the French-speaking enclave at court, Edward's promotion of his continental friends remained low key and did not challenge the earls or other prominent landowners in England.

At the end of the 1040s, relations between Edward and Godwine deteriorated. Earl Swein was banished in 1047 and again in 1049 (for the murder of King Swein's brother) and divisions appeared within Godwine's family. Other causes of contention included Godwine's marriage of his third son Tostig to Judith of Flanders in opposition to Edward's new alliance with Saxony. In 1050 Edward promoted the Norman Robert of Jumièges to the see of Canterbury in preference to Godwine's candidate, and sent him to Rome for the *pallium,* the archbishop's stole, which it was a papal privilege to bestow. Edward may have been mindful of Godwine's legendary greed and the need to promote an archbishop who would resist his territorial ambitions in Kent.

By the spring of 1051 tensions were acute and, despite efforts at compromise, little was needed to bring matters to a head. Confrontation was sparked by a fraças at Dover between Edward's brother-in-law Eustace of Boulogne and men of the town whom Godwine refused to discipline. Both sides assembled forces but Godwine's supporters were unwilling to confront the king. With their forces crumbling, Godwine and his family fled abroad, variously to Flanders and Dublin. The collapse of Godwine's power was dramatic. As one contemporary remarked: 'he was formerly so very much raised up, as if he ruled the king and all England; and his sons were earls and the king's favourites'.

Edward had triumphed, therefore, and set about rewarding his allies. Leofric's son Aelfgar obtained East Anglia, Odda of Deerhurst was made earl in western Wessex and a Frenchman was promoted to London. Edward clearly intended that no one figure should replace Godwine. Instead, 1051 presented him with an opportunity for his own personal rule. One version of the *Anglo-Saxon Chronicle* mentions a visit to Edward by Duke William in 1051, and William of Poitiers later claimed that Archbishop Robert carried Edward's offer of the English succession to Normandy. Henry I of France certainly rounded on his long-time protégé in 1052 and invaded Normandy, and the English succession may well have been the reason. Henry apparently sided thereafter with Godwine. Certainty eludes us but it does seem likely that Edward sent Godwine's youngest son and grandson to William in 1051 and made an offer of sorts concerning the succession, in expectation of Norman assistance against Godwine. It may be that William's emergence in 1050 to effective control of Normandy helped condition the timing of Edward's confrontation with Godwine.

If that was Edward's thinking, it came to naught since French and Angevin hostility kept William at home. Godwine outmanoeuvred Earls Odda and Ralph in the Channel, joined Harold at Portland and raised the men of Sussex, where his family's influence was greatest. King and earl confronted one another at London in the late summer of 1052. Again there was no fighting but Godwine had the upper hand and it was Edward who had to concede, admitting back in full Godwine, Edith and Harold. Robert and other Norman bishops fled England, Odda was set aside and Edward's personal rule was undone. Swein died on pilgrimage in 1052 and Godwine himself at court in 1053, but Harold thereafter succeeded to his father's dominating position in southern England and the court.

After 1052 Edward had little room for manoeuvre and only the building of an ostentatiously Norman-style monastery at Westminster was clearly his own initiative. This was modelled on Jumièges and other monastic churches in and around Rouen and reflects his continuing interest in the Norman connection. But beneath the king, the council was increasingly dominated by Harold and his clerical allies (including Stigand who had now added Canterbury to Winchester), who did not share Edward's appetite for continental connections.

The regime was, however, united in promoting Edward's interests within Britain. Earl Siward successfully intervened in Scotland against Macbeth in 1054 and placed Malcolm on the throne. Siward probably took this opportunity to consolidate his own control of Cumbria, where the tower at Morland provides an example of late Anglo-Saxon work. However, Siward died the following year and the council promoted Harold's brother Tostig to Northumbria, and outlawed Earl Aelfgar, Leofric's son, perhaps because he had objected. This gave Godwine's sons two of the three most powerful English earldoms and oversight of the Scottish border.

By 1055 Gruffudd ap Llywelyn was king of all Wales and in a position to challenge for control of the Marches. He and the exiled Aelfgar defeated Earl Ralph and sacked Hereford, and Gruffudd went on to kill Harold's appointee as bishop there in 1056. Harold and Leofric negotiated a peace by which Aelfgar was restored to East Anglia, while Gruffudd recognized Edward as his overlord in return for English acknowledgement of his own pan-Welsh kingship. Harold added Herefordshire to his own earldom.

The partnership of the houses of Godwine and Cerdic which characterized the 1050s and 1060s proved highly successful: the rulers of both Wales and Scotland (in 1059) acknowledged Edward's lordship, so restoring English kingship to the heights of Edgar's reign. England had enjoyed a lengthy freedom from Viking attacks and the regime had delivered widespread peace and prosperity at home. Edward was in many respects well served by his earls, yet it must be noted that Harold's position was becoming ever more firmly entrenched as the 'under-king' and principal executive of the king, as well as his brother-in-law.

The deaths of Earls Leofric and Ralph in 1057 removed significant rivals. Aelfgar obtained Leofric's Mercia but had to relinquish East Anglia, which Harold secured for his brother Gyrth, to add to his existing tenure of Oxfordshire. At some date, another brother, Leofwine, was given an earldom in Middlesex and Hertfordshire and Siward's son, Waltheof, was given an earldom in the south-east Midlands but he was of little political importance before the Conquest. Aelfgar therefore obtained Mercia but was surrounded by the earldoms of the Godwinesons. Only in Wales had he political allies, where Gruffudd became his son-in-law. Two opposing factions existed, therefore, around 1060, but there can be no doubt which was dominant both militarily and in terms of access to royal patronage.

Although the deaths of Henry I and Count Geoffrey Martel in 1060 and the succession to both of minors deprived Harold of his natural allies on the continent, in England his power continued to increase. Earl Aelfgar seems to have died about 1062 and the appointment of his young and inexperienced son Edwin to Mercia enabled Harold and Tostig to invade and destroy the kingship of Gruffudd in Wales. They then established new rulers under Harold's own superior lordship. Godwine's sons now held all England as earls, excepting only Mercia, with Scotland under Tostig's ally, Malcolm, and Wales subservient to Harold. Including Queen Edith, the estates of the Godwinesons exceeded in value those of the king and their collective power arguably overreached his.

By the 1060s Edward had lost the power to make his own appointments to both secular and clerical positions where those were opposed by the Godwine family *en masse.* The pattern of landholding in 1066 betrays something of this disempowerment, with Tostig, for example, still holding strategic estates in the Isle of Wight long after his appointment to Northumbria. The desire of powerful families to pass on their offices to family members prevailed in Wessex and Mercia under Edward, but the balance between several families which Edward inherited had disintegrated. The four brothers of the queen held earldoms that collectively controlled the interface between royal power and regional communities across three-quarters of England, and they and their allies formed the largest group within the king's council. Harold and Tostig clearly predominated. The author of the *Life of King Edward* wrote of them:

> These two great brothers of a cloud-born land,
> The kingdom's sacred oaks, two Hercules,
> Excel all Englishmen when joined in peace;

By the time this was penned, Harold and Tostig had ceased to co-operate and both were dead. In the author's view, it was this above all else which had caused heaven to fall in and foes to cross English bounds in triumph. His view has some weight.

FOUR

An Heir to King Edward

The accession of a bachelor king already some thirty-seven years old in 1042 meant that the succession was never far from the political agenda throughout the reign. Cnut had died at about that age and both his sons significantly younger. Edward was unlikely to reign long enough to enable a grown son to succeed him, and that concern can only have deepened as the years passed and Edith – Godwine's daughter whom Edward married in 1045 – failed to show any signs of conceiving. During the 1040s Godwine may well have looked to the prospect of ruling England during the minority of his own grandson but, if so, such hopes were necessarily receding by the end of the decade. Edward's later reputation for sanctity has encouraged the view that he was a celibate and his *Life* depicts his relationship with Edith as one more like father and daughter. Perhaps Edward was loathe to provide Godwine –

whom he suspected of complicity in his brother's death – with a royal grandchild. Even so, he probably did attempt to provide for the succession. His disposal of Edith in 1051 into a nunnery may imply that he then intended to remarry and try again but the return to power of her father and brothers in 1052 debarred any such plans. Edward eventually died without issue and it must have long been clear that this was the likeliest outcome.

Several factors influenced the selection of a king in late Anglo-Saxon England. Candidates were invariably male, and adults had by far the best chance. Royal kinship was important: with the exception of Swein I, whose royalty derived from the Danish line, every king since Alfred had been a son of a king of England, so effective candidacy was clearly conditioned by paternal descent. The attitudes of leading churchmen were also important, particularly as coronation was performed by archbishops and bishops, while secular political opinion – including the views of earls and other royal officers – was also significant. When feasible, candidates reinforced their claims via their maternal and marital kindreds, their tenants and regional support.

Most potent of all, however, was royal nomination of a successor. Kings normally named close relatives and most often sons if such were available. The old king's preference was accorded weight by all concerned. Edward's was crucial to the candidacies of both William and Harold.

Despite the large family sired by his father, Edward had few close relatives. His only full brother, Alfred, had died during the crisis following Cnut's death. His half-brothers were long dead and only Edmund had produced offspring. The regime negotiated the return of Edmund's son, Edward the Exile, from Hungary, presumably as a potential successor, but he died on arrival in England in 1057, 'to the misfortune of this wretched nation', leaving an infant son – Edgar the Atheling – and two daughters. In 1066 Edgar alone could legitimately lay claim to the lineage of Cerdic as Edmund Ironside's grandson. Yet he was only about fourteen and his immediate kin were foreigners without influence or a following capable of pressing his candidacy. Only the committed support of the earls and Edward could have delivered Edgar the throne and this was not forthcoming.

Edward did have close kin through his sister, who

produced sons by her marriage to Dreux of the
Vexin. One, Ralph the Timid, followed Edward to
England and was married into a prominent East
Midland family and promoted to an earldom, only
to die in 1057, leaving a child, Harold. Walter, who
succeeded to the Vexin, fell foul of Duke William
when he attempted to make himself count also of
Maine and died in prison at Falaise. Whether
contemporaries in England saw either as a potential
candidate seems unlikely. There was little precedent
for succession via female descent and Edward does
not seem to have marked them as potential heirs.

In Denmark there was another candidate, Swein
Estrithsson, who was Cnut's nephew and the
grandson of Swein I, both of whom had been kings
in England. Swein's candidacy may have been
favoured by the Godwine family in default of a son
to Edith during the 1040s, and the presence of his
brother Beorn in England might then have been
significant, but Beorn's murder by Godwine's eldest
son ended any prospect that they would willingly
support Swein's candidacy and war with Norway kept
him away.

In Norway, Magnus may have considered he had
some claim to England by virtue of an agreement

reputedly made between himself and Harthacnut in about 1039, which provided for the inheritance of each to fall to the other should either die childless, as Harthacnut did. However, Magnus died in 1047. His successor, the legendary Harald Hardrada, had interests in the British Isles and may well have been seeking allies capable of providing support for an attempt on the throne when he dispatched a fleet to the Irish Sea in 1058. This force clearly impressed Welsh commentators and was active in support of Gruffudd and Aelfgar, and against Earl Harold, but neither of these principles survived to 1066. When Hardrada's armada then set out for the conquest of England, his strategy was essentially opportunistic and he could not expect any allies inside southern Britain.

Having spent so much of his own life in Normandy, Edward had good reason to recall his father's Anglo-Norman alliance and may have considered William's candidacy a viable solution to England's vulnerability to Scandinavian attack. Once William had emerged as an effective ruler – in the very late 1040s – it may have been Edward's intention that the duke should succeed him on the English throne. William's apologists later made much of Edward's nomination and there is just sufficient non-partisan evidence to take the claim seriously. There can be little doubt that William projected himself as Edward's nominated successor and he clearly entertained strong ambitions to succeed.

Yet few of Edward's subjects had good reason to share his enthusiasm for a Norman candidate. The senior aristocracy had either been put in place by Scandinavian kings or had accommodated them. The prospect of a Norman king supported by warriors greedy for English estates and offices can only have alarmed them. Furthermore, William's credentials were unimpressive: his bastardy cannot have endeared him to the prelates, while his connection with Edward was via the latter's mother, Emma, who was his great-aunt and not his paternal kin, so that his claims to royal descent were nebulous. Nor did the Viking threat seem pressing by 1060, following two decades that had witnessed only brief and small-scale raids. Few could still recall the massed Scandinavian attacks that had typified the latter part of Aethelred's reign and driven Edward himself into exile.

In southern England, therefore, the ruling classes

had good reason to look to an insular successor who would defend their property and offices. Even so, there was arguably profound difference of opinion as to whom that should be. Once Edward the Exile was dead, the elite had necessarily to look outside Edward's close kin for candidates. This opened the way for Earl Harold to construct his own candidacy. Harold was for over a decade the most powerful figure in England beneath the king and was Edward's brother-in-law – and there were tenth-century precedents for such a relationship helping to legitimize the seizure of English kingships. It is unclear when this objective began to crystallize but he may well have had ambitions concerning the throne for several years before 1066.

The earliest context in which Harold's ambitions become to an extent visible lies in his putative and undated visit to Normandy, which was so graphically recorded on the Bayeux Tapestry but went unmentioned in any English source. In essence, the story goes that Harold crossed to Ponthieu from Bosham in Sussex but was there imprisoned by Count Guy and only released by the intervention of Duke William. Following a successful campaign with the duke against Brittany, Harold was knighted and committed himself on oath to William's candidacy for the English succession. The Brittany campaign seems to fix this story in the period 1064–5 but the purpose of Harold's journey remains obscure and there is scant reason to accept Norman claims that Harold was sent by Edward to confirm his earlier nomination. As Eadmer later suggested, Harold may have sought the release of his brother and nephew who were still in custody in Normandy. The Tapestry implies that Edward was angered by the result, and this can only mean by Harold's oath.

The visit did, however, provide an opportunity for the two principal candidates to meet and discuss issues of mutual interest, and some sort of agreement seems to have been made by which William was to receive the throne while Harold's position was secured by a double marriage alliance and 'everything which you ask of me which can reasonably be granted'. In the recent history of the succession there was nothing exceptional about such an arrangement, although Harold had no right in law to make such arrangements without the express approval of King Edward – and such was clearly lacking.

His own candidacy does, however, seem to have

influenced Harold when faced by a crisis within England in the autumn of 1065, when the Northumbrians rose in revolt against Earl Tostig. Contemporary sources suggest that Tostig had attempted to increase taxation on the north, had misused the legal system as a means of acquiring wealth and had murdered several opponents. The northerners demanded he be replaced, ransacked Tostig's headquarters at York and marched south where they ravaged Northamptonshire. Their choice of successor was Leofric's younger grandson, Morcar, and the rebels were joined by Edwin of Mercia.

Edward's reaction was to order a mobilization and outface his opponents but various of his councillors – necessarily including Harold – undermined this process. Instead Harold acted as go-between and negotiated what was, from Edward's perspective, an ignominious climb-down. The northerners obtained Morcar as titular earl, which meant that they could effectively expect to rule themselves. Tostig and his wife were forced into exile and left for Flanders, laden with treasure by King Edward. The old king died a few weeks later and Harold secured the throne. Thereafter the fact emerged that he had married the sister of Edwin and Morcar.

By contrast with his earlier campaigns on behalf of
Edward's kingship, in Wales for example, Harold's
behaviour in 1065 seems timorous. An explanation
might be that he considered a *rapprochement* with
Leofric's grandsons of greater benefit to himself
than support for Tostig, who was clearly favoured by
Queen Edith and may also have been uncomfortably
close to Edward. If Harold saw himself as a potential
candidate for the throne so too was Tostig, and this
may have been decisive. The outcome rid him of a
potential rival, whom Edward might have nominated
and who could expect both Flemish and Scottish
support. Alternatively, Tostig might have thrown his
support behind the young Edgar, or even William,
and so undermined Harold's candidacy – we cannot
know. At the same time Harold secured the
commitment of Leofric's grandsons to his own
ambitions. It is little wonder that Tostig accused
Harold before the king of complicity with the rebels,
a charge from which he cleared himself on oath. But
as the author of the *Life of King Edward* remarked,
'Harold was rather too generous with oaths (alas!)'.

The ailing Edward journeyed 'towards midwinter'
to his magnificent new monastic church at Westminster, which was consecrated on 28 December,

FIVE

1066

On the morning of 5 January 1066 the coffin containing the corporal remains of Edward the Confessor were laid to rest in Westminster Abbey. In the afternoon, Harold II was crowned king of England. Despite adverse comment in Norman literature, Harold had been nominated by his predecessor and had the support of a broad cross-section of the English élite. He was probably crowned by Archbishop Ealdred of York, given the controversies already surrounding the legitimacy of Stigand's tenure of Canterbury, which had led several of Edward's bishops to seek consecration abroad.

The new regime was in many respects formidable. Harold was in his mid-thirties, with two decades of successful political and military experience behind him. He was brother-in-law to his predecessor and descended on the maternal side from the outer echelons of Denmark's royal family. He had sons and brothers in some numbers, and either had recently tied, or now tied, to himself by marriage the only family in England capable of rivalling his own. He was himself the head of the largest and most expansive system of patronage in England, and the combination of his own lands and patronage with those of the crown offered the prospect of a revitalized kingship, wealthier and more powerful than for several generations. A crowned head accompanied by a sceptre on his new coinage proclaimed his kingship and the reverse motif 'Pacx' signalled his aspirations.

In the early months of the year Harold sought acceptance of his kingship. He wore his crown at York, where the Northumbrians may have been chary of supporting Tostig's brother, and dispatched messengers to Normandy. In late spring he mobilized a large force of ships and men to defend the south coast against Norman attack but it was Tostig who appeared first. With ships provided by Baldwin of Flanders Tostig descended on the Isle of Wight, where he had numerous estates, and raised money and supplies prior to raiding coastal Sussex and Kent, where he recruited support. Before

Harold could reach the area from London, Tostig sailed north to the Humber and struck at Lindsey with a force reputedly of sixty ships. Edwin and Morcar drove him off and Tostig's forces disintegrated. His Flemish and southern English followers turned south but Tostig and his closest supporters sailed to Scotland to King Malcolm.

It is unclear what Tostig hoped to achieve. His was not a full-scale invasion. He may have hoped to make of himself a sufficient nuisance to persuade Harold to readmit him to his estates, as prominent figures had done repeatedly during recent reigns. Unfortunately for him, Harold could not afford to risk alienating Edwin and Morcar or Northumbrian opinion. Additionally, he was himself presumably profiting from control of the bulk of Tostig's estates. In these circumstances, the English leaders closed ranks and Tostig was forced to pursue his ambitions by other means.

Tostig's next opportunity came with the arrival in Scottish waters of a Viking armada under the command of Harald Hardrada of Norway. The Scandinavians took the island route to Britain, collecting reinforcements in the Orkneys and Shetlands, and seem to have achieved a measure of surprise. Harold Godwineson was obliged by supply problems to stand down his forces on 8 September, having deterred invasion throughout the bulk of the fighting season and perhaps even driven off Norman operations in the Channel. Soon after, the Norwegians sailed into the Tyne with a force reckoned variously at 300 and 500 ships. Tostig allied himself to Harald, submitted to him and became his man, and his status as a Godwineson and a member of Edward's regime brought Hardrada some badly needed credibility inside England.

The Norwegians entered the Humber and the Ouse, disembarking on about 16 September to attack York, the principal fortress and only major town and governmental centre in northern England. York appears to have closed its gates to the Scandinavians and awaited relief; the town's resistance may have been stiffened by the presence of Tostig, the earl whom the townsfolk had themselves expelled only twelve months before. Earls Edwin and Morcar reached York only a few days later and fought against the Norwegian host at Gate Fulford, within sight of the walls, on 20 September.

Why Edwin and Morcar chose to fight rather than

await Harold II in the comparative safety of York is unclear, although it must be said that victory had the potential to enhance massively their standing within the regime. They lost the battle, however, and suffered significant casualties as their forces sought the safety of the west bank of the Ouse. The battle finished Morcar as earl of Northumbria and seriously weakened his and Edwin's military credibility.

York surrendered to Hardrada and the Yorkshiremen provisioned his forces and agreed to join him; then the Norwegians withdrew to Stamford Bridge, on the borders of the North and East Ridings, to await hostages. Harold II had been alerted to Hardrada's attack soon after his descent on England. He mobilized troops at great speed and marched north, reaching Tadcaster on Sunday 24 September. On the Monday, Harold led his forces through York to Stamford Bridge – a distance of 26 kilometres – and there surprised and decisively defeated his enemies. Both Hardrada and Tostig fell. Just twenty-four ships were reputedly sufficient to transport home those who survived the rout and long pursuit.

Stamford Bridge was a decisive victory that

brought huge kudos to Harold II, whose kingship was vastly reinforced by this apparent display of divine approval. From the perspective of those supporting his candidacy, the new king had amply justified their choice and proved himself the greatest soldier-king of the English since Edmund Ironside. Harold's campaign in Yorkshire had, however, left open the southern coast of England to invasion, and William's fleet finally dropped anchor at Pevensey on 28 September.

William had spent the spring and summer preparing for his own invasion. He apparently obtained the support of Pope Alexander III and Swein of Denmark for his claim, and made a defensive pact with Henry IV of Saxony. However, none of these agreements brought him significant reinforcements. More important was William's own superiority over other counts along the Atlantic coast and the minorities of potential enemies, particularly Philip I of France and the Count of Anjou, either of whom might otherwise have threatened Normandy in his absence.

At home, William may have had some difficulty persuading his vassals of the viability of his plans but a fleet was constructed and concentrated on the

Dives estuary and he mobilized an army there. Soldiers were recruited from Normandy and also from Brittany, Flanders and elsewhere in France, serving in the expectation of pay and reward. It is unclear whether William then despaired of the southerly wind needed to carry his forces to England from Dives and launched his flotilla in less than favourable conditions or actually decided to relocate to the Somme, but there the fleet was trapped until the onset of favourable weather in late September.

The lateness of the season allowed William to embark in the knowledge that the English navy was no longer poised in the Solent to cut off his retreat once he had disembarked, but his crossing was far from smooth-running and his rapid move from Pevensey to Hastings suggests that he had landed further west than intended. At both places he threw up castles and then set about ravaging Sussex, where Harold's hereditary estates and tenants were concentrated. His later punishment of the men of Romney for resisting his foragers demonstrates that local opinion was hostile to the Norman army. William's forces had necessarily to live off the land: Harold, in contrast, could not act similarly yet at the same time pose as England's defender.

William's arrival was probably reported to Harold within a few days and may, if he had not already left Yorkshire, have precipitated his march south. News of Stamford Bridge seems to have reached William early in October, and may have encouraged him to remain close to the sea. However, both seem to have sought battle, and this has occasioned much later comment. Harold has been widely criticized for his impetuosity in the Hasting's campaign, his failure to raise larger forces, his eventual loss of the initiative and his reputed tactical errors, but much of this can be attributed to his defeat and death. Decisive battles were a rarity at the time but Harold had himself been victorious in one against a far more famous foe just weeks earlier, had good reason to be confident and was leading troops buoyed up by success. William, by contrast, had no experience of pitched battle but had fought numerous sieges. Harold was personally acquainted with Norman tactics but not vice versa. If Harold did dispatch his ships from London to attack William's, as William of Poitiers asserts, an uncomplicated land advance and immediate attack were obligatory, given the lateness of the season.

The battle of Hastings took place on 14 October

some 10 kilometres north of Hastings, on the site since graced by Battle Abbey. The conflict was hard-fought, with substantial losses on both sides. French sources, including the Bayeux Tapestry, provide considerable detail concerning the battle, much of which may well have been developed in retrospect to project an image of William as a brilliant leader of men. Critical, however, were the deaths of Harold and his brothers, Leofwine and Gyrth. English kings had lost battles before and survived: these deaths removed the figures around whom the regime was constructed and undermined the very legitimacy of Harold's rule.

News of the defeat at Hastings was both a military and a psychological blow to the councillors at London. Faced by such proof of God's intervention against the Godwinesons, Archbishop Ealdred and his colleagues regrouped around Edgar's candidacy, attracted presumably by the indubitable legitimacy conferred by his descent from the line of Cerdic. There was no shortage of soldiery: the Londoners backed Edgar and others flocked in. The problem was offering them credible leadership. Edgar was an inexperienced boy and Harold's sons and nephews were little older. No other figure in southern

England had a military reputation or experience of command. The credibility of Earls Edwin and Morcar and their followers had been undermined by defeat at Gate Fulford and their leadership is unlikely to have been acceptable in the south. Edgar was active as king for several weeks following Hastings but his supporters did little more than gather at London.

The initiative lay, therefore, with William, who buried the dead and garrisoned Hastings. When the English proved no more amenable to his candidacy he secured Dover, which had featured in earlier negotiations with Harold. Thence the Normans, by now suffering from dysentery, marched on Canterbury, which capitulated unfought, then up Watling Street to Southwark, where English soldiers were repulsed across London Bridge and houses fired. The Norman army then marched west and crossed the Thames at Wallingford, while still raiding widely to support itself and undermine the morale of its enemies.

English opposition began to collapse at this juncture. Archbishop Stigand was the first to surrender to William. Edgar's embryonic regime was doomed by his failure to mobilize a credible force capable of relieving such of England's numerous walled centres as William attacked. Edgar and his supporters surrendered to William at Berkhamsted, at which point the Norman army had effectively cut off London from Edwin's Mercia. The Normans then took over London, despite some evidence of further, abortive resistance, and began the construction of the White Tower.

Amid chaotic scenes, William was crowned king of the English by Archbishop Ealdred of York at Westminster on Christmas Day 1066. For the moment, at least, his coronation resolved the issue of England's kingship after a tumultuous year and offered an opportunity for reconciliation to begin.

SIX

A Conquest Consolidated

In Westminster Abbey, on Christmas Day 1066, William solemnly swore on the Bible that he would 'hold this nation as well as the best of any kings before him did, if they would be loyal to him'. The principal English leaders had already submitted to him, sought his commendation and sworn him oaths, and opportunities were presented soon after for other men to submit and acknowledge him as king: a general submission of the Mercians occurred at Barking in January, others did homage at Pevensey in March and opportunities were made available for lesser men to do so in their own localities. There seems every reason to think that both sides sought accommodation. William's early behaviour as king contrasts to an extent with that of Cnut in 1016 in somewhat similar circumstances, in that there was no vendetta against the old English royal family nor proscription of leading figures.

Rather, Edgar was honoured as a close kinsman. Although they are unidentified, contemporaries claimed that he was provided with wide estates and that English land-tenure was generally confirmed. Prominent among the survivors of the English establishment in the south were Edward's court officers such as Azur, formerly his steward, and his several French courtiers. Local administration necessarily continued for several years in the hands of English or anglicized reeves and officials, whose knowledge of procedure and law was essential to the new regime. So too did Englishmen continue to defend their localities. Eadnoth the Staller, for example, was killed leading local thegns against Harold's son, Godwine, on the southern shores of the Bristol Channel in 1068.

There were, of course, important exceptions to this picture. Other than Queen Edith and perhaps Countess Gytha, Godwine's family and their closest associates were dispossessed, and this placed vast estates in East Anglia, the home counties, Wessex and Herefordshire in the hands of the king. These lands massively augmented existing royal resources and enabled William's rapid redistribution of land to his Norman and French associates, many of whom obtained strategically important holdings and custody of newly constructed castles. William expected English landholders who submitted to him both to do homage and to pay a large fine, and even those with extensive resources found the latter condition onerous. The complaint was made that men were expected to buy back their lands. Few details are available but Abbot Brand of Peterborough paid £240. His burden may have been punitive since Peterborough's then abbot had been with Harold at Hastings and Brand had then sought Edgar's commendation, but figures of this size would have been ruinous to many landholders. Such men pledged their lands and then lost them when they failed to repay debts and several abbeys obtained new estates by this means.

When the king then levied a heavy geld early in 1067 to pay his troops, some may have found themselves unable to pay, and William seems to have sanctioned their dispossession by anyone who was prepared to make the necessary contribution. Since gelds were levied almost yearly during the reign, this became a potent means by which incomers could acquire land, since they were the recipients of much of William's largesse and so were better able to afford his taxes. William's well-publicized liberality as a patron of clerics and soldiers was necessarily dependant on much-increased levels of taxation upon his new subjects.

Like Cnut before him, William initially relied heavily on his closest associates and placed considerable responsibilities – and commensurate resources – in their hands. Overall control of Harold's old earldom was divided between William fitzOsbern, who obtained the central south, the south-west and Herefordshire, and Odo, Bishop of Bayeux, who took over Kent, where he obtained many of the estates of Aethelnoth of Canterbury. Both were responsible for establishing their own followers on English estates, although the chronology is only rarely discernible. Alongside them, the king also enfeoffed others of his friends, for example establishing Hugh de Montfort at Dover Castle.

By March 1067 William was sufficiently confident of his position to return to Normandy in triumph. He took with him some of the more prominent of his new English subjects, including Archbishop Stigand, Edgar, Edwin, Morcar and Waltheof. Opinion is now divided as to his motives for their attendance but their absence from England may well have been considered necessary to his security, and Orderic Vitalis described them as effectively hostages. William left England in the keeping of Odo and fitzOsbern, who 'built castles widely throughout this nation, and oppressed the wretched people'. The absence of the king and key members of the English élite for nine months certainly provided conditions ideal for Norman aggrandizement and this arguably had a damaging impact on English confidence in William's kingship. Since 1035 English kings had not absented themselves and the rapid revival of journeying overseas now set up new problems of governance which needed to be addressed.

During William's absence there were sporadic disturbances against his dispositions. He had appointed Copsi, Tostig's former lieutenant and an Anglo-Dane from Yorkshire, to the earldom of Northumberland, but he was murdered by the local claimant to that title, Osulf of Bamburgh, on his arrival north of the Tyne. Northerners had successfully imposed their own preferences regarding the earldom on Edward in 1065 and they now apparently assumed that William was as open to persuasion. Copsi was clearly an impolitic appointee by a king who had yet to come to grips with the complexities of northern politics.

In the Welsh Marches, Eadric the Wild – a nephew of Eadric Streona – allied himself with King Bleddyn of Gwynedd and attacked the garrison at Hereford. His purpose is unclear but he may well have been heading opposition to the depredations of the Norman castellans. In Kent, Edward's brother-in-law, Eustace Count of Boulogne, attacked Dover castle but was beaten off by the garrison. William of Poitiers suggested that the Kentish thegns invited Eustace in and offered him their support for the kingship but, whatever their several objectives, the episode proved a fiasco. Both Eadric and Eustace were later reconciled with William and it has recently been suggested that the issues in each case may have been comparatively personal. However, such actions were symptomatic of the unpopularity of Norman garrisons.

In April the Penitential Ordinance was published in Normandy, establishing levels of penance appropriate to violence committed within the different phases of the Conquest. A central feature was the assumption that William's opponents throughout 1066, even before his coronation, were rebels, and this reflects the platform on which his regime was increasingly to be based. William's return in December provided an opportunity for the implications of the Ordinance to disseminate, to the discomfiture of the English. Despite the king's sale of the northern earldom to Gospatric of Bamburgh, incomers then secured other appointments, including the see of Dorchester. By the end of 1067, it was becoming clear that William would favour Normans over indigenous candidates for promotion in the church. In this respect there is an important contrast with Cnut, who necessarily recruited heavily from Englishmen for clerical appointments. In addition, William gave Normans special protection *vis-à-vis* the English by the imposition of heavy, communal fines for killing them, so giving the unpopular garrison troops increased security.

In the heartland of Harold's hereditary lands, particularly in Sussex but also elsewhere, William set about establishing a series of new castleries. This led to an extensive reorganization of lordship and land-tenure, with the refocusing of lordship on to new castles, such as William de Warenne's at Lewes. The king was understandably interested in control of the south-east and communication with Normandy but into open defiance. Early in the year Exeter closed its gates; William promptly besieged the city for eighteen days until a settlement was negotiated. Countess Gytha's presence and the fact that Exeter was part of Queen Edith's dower may mean that the House of Godwine played some part in this act of defiance. The *Anglo-Saxon Chronicle* suggested that the townsfolk surrendered because 'the thegns had betrayed them': Gytha was a prominent landholder in the region and Harold's son Godwine arrived in the Bristol Channel with an Irish-Norse fleet later that summer. Although he was driven off, it may be that there was a concerted attempt by the family to regain influence and even challenge William, which collapsed when its separate parts were individually suppressed. The recruitment of allies certainly suggests that the Exeter rising was premeditated. If there was a conspiracy, however, it was poorly co-ordinated. William constructed Rougemont Castle, which thereafter dominated Exeter, and distributed further Devon estates to trusted followers, so bringing new castles and honors such as Totnes into existence. Although the men of Exeter were not severely punished, this episode significantly increased Norman penetration into the region. It also contributed to a critical decline in the mutual confidence of both William and the English regarding the intentions of the other.

Among those who chose to depart from England were Countess Gytha 'and the wives of many good men with her', who eventually found refuge in Flanders and France. More important was the departure of the enigmatic figure of Maerleswein. If all the references to this name in Domesday Book are to a single individual, he was an important nobleman with extensive estates in various parts of England, including the south-west, but most particularly in the north midlands and Yorkshire, where he had served as sheriff of Lincolnshire. Maerleswein held lands from King Edward in Somerset and had widespread estates in Cornwall, with a total of 160 ploughlands, all of which had passed to the Count of Mortain by 1086. William campaigned in Cornwall after the surrender of Exeter, so it is likely that Maerleswein's flight to Scotland was a direct consequence of the failure of a wider conspiracy in the south-west. Maerleswein's status and lands require that he was a significant and widely connected figure in late Anglo-Saxon England, and it seems quite possible that he was at the centre of whatever resistance to William was being planned.

With Maerleswein went 'many good men' and Edgar the Atheling and his sisters. Their departure from southern England during the spring of 1068 marks the point at which English dissatisfaction regarding William's kingship had become so serious among key sections of the English élite that they had resolved to act against him. For them the honeymoon period was over and the candidacy of Prince Edgar had regained its attractions.

Despite these defections, William proceeded with plans to consolidate his political position and involve English as well as Norman leaders in his kingship. As Orderic remarked, many Englishmen kept faith with the king. In May 1068 William's wife Matilda was crowned queen at Westminster by Archbishop Ealdred. Among those whose names were appended to two charters written at this date were the Anglo-Saxon earls, Edwin, Morcar and Waltheof, as well as other lesser figures. Their presence meant that William could still in the early summer of 1068 reasonably claim to be fulfilling his coronation oath as regards his new subjects.

Despite rising discontent, open opposition to William was limited. Different groups of critics arguably had contrary objectives. The Godwine family may have preferred their own candidate for the throne, while Maerleswein clearly supported Edgar. Others sent to Denmark to invite in Cnut's heirs. There again, the English, and particularly the bishops, were deeply monarchist in sentiment and in broad terms conformist. In Wessex and East Anglia at least, the desire to make accommodation work was for many, most of the time, more powerful than the urge to turn complaint into revolt. Having only recently submitted and sworn oaths to William, there was a general unwillingness to confront him in arms, particularly given his military reputation following the events of 1066. Such considerations conditioned reactions to his rule and militated against wholesale rebellion, at least in the south where English kingship was most deeply entrenched.

SEVEN

Revolt and its Suppression in the North

During 1067 the English aristocracy in Wessex, East Anglia and the Home Counties had come under severe pressure and many estates had passed into Norman hands. Elsewhere, English tenure remained the rule, excepting only Herefordshire. There the garrisons of William fitzOsbern and others already established there by Edward, such as Richard fitzScrob at Richard's Castle, were making inroads. Within a few months of Matilda's coronation in May 1068, however, Earls Edwin and Morcar abandoned King William and went into open opposition.

The reasons for their about-face are unclear and the matter is poorly represented in even near-contemporary literature. Roger of Montgomery had come to England with William in December 1067 and was rapidly established by the king at Chichester and Arundel. His appointment as Earl of Shrewsbury may have occurred soon after, although it is generally dated to 1071. If it were earlier, Edwin presumably opposed his construction of a castle within his own area of influence. Additionally it was about now that William gave executive powers in Mercia to the abbot of Evesham, which may have undermined the earl's position. However, Orderic Vitalis remarked that Edwin had been disappointed that an earlier promise of marriage to William's daughter had come to naught. This would have given Edwin a position within William's regime comparable to that which his sister's marriage to Harold II had once offered him. Earl Waltheof – a rival for William's favour from within the old English leadership – obtained the hand of the king's niece, Judith, and this Edwin may well have resented. Orderic represented Edwin as having been granted authority over Mercia, which was 'almost a third of England', alongside this offer of marriage, so he had every reason to consider himself the senior figure of the two. Orderic then had him allying himself with Bleddyn of Gwynedd, whom he wrongly represented as Edwin's nephew (he was the maternal half-brother of that Gruffudd ap Llywelyn same time, Maerleswein's espousal of Edgar in the spring of 1068 necessarily impacted upon opinion in Lincolnshire and Yorkshire. The House of Leofric was less well established in the east midlands than in the west. Maerleswein was sheriff of Lincolnshire in 1066 and held estates with more than fifty ploughlands in the shire in addition to his recent receipt of the extensive lands of one Grimketill, against whom charges were then outstanding. Maeleswein does seem from the Kesteven claims attached to Domesday Book to have been, as sheriff, operating outside strict regard for the law but even so his championing of Edgar during 1067 made him a prominent figure inside Mercia at the very time that his involvement in the Exeter affair is likely to have led to royal demands to sequester his estates. For several reasons, therefore, the earl may have felt obliged to place himself at the head of Mercian opposition to William rather than be seen as the local agent of an increasingly unpopular regime.

It is unclear how widely Edwin's rising spread. In 1066 he and his brother had demonstrated an ability to act fast and decisively but those qualities were not visible in 1068. Orderic again:

After large numbers of the leading men of England and Wales had met together, a general outcry arose against the injustice and tyranny which the Normans and their comrades-in-arms had inflicted on the English. They sent envoys into every corner of Britain to incite men openly and secretly against the enemy. All were ready to conspire together to recover their former liberty, and bind themselves by weighty oaths against the Normans. In the regions north of the Humber violent disturbances broke out. The rebels prepared to defend themselves in woods, marshes and creeks, and in some cities. The city of York was seething with discontent, and showed no respect for the holy office of its archbishop when he tried to appease it.

Despite Welsh support, Edwin seems not to have mobilized an adequate army before William marched into the midlands in strength, constructing and garrisoning castles at Warwick and Nottingham. At that point the insurrection collapsed. Only Orderic referred to this enterprise and precedent would suggest that real enthusiasm for a risky initiative headed by Leofric's grandsons would be confined to north-western Mercia, Northumbria and North Wales. Nor does this account read like an attempt to undo William's kingship. Rather, the

English intention seems to have been to negotiate with the king from strength rather than to fight. Even so, Orderic did describe the rebellion as a 'fierce insurrection'.

In Northumbria, revolt had other causes. The wooing of Edgar's sister, Margaret, by Malcolm of Scotland (they married in 1070) gave the Atheling and his supporters a comparatively safe refuge from which they could foment rebellion in the north. The stress laid on Margaret's lineage from Edgar the Peaceable and the Emperor Henry by contemporary chroniclers emphasizes Edgar's own legitimacy as a royal candidate. Furthermore, it raised the possibility that the disenchanted northerners might accede to Malcolm's kingship and effectively secede from England. In the face of this, Archbishop Ealdred seems to have failed in attempts to manage a general submission to William and the men of York backed Edwin and Morcar. However, William's appearance in force at Nottingham led the men of the northern capital to lose their collective nerve and sue for peace, and there followed a general pacification which included Archill, the wealthy Yorkshire thegn, and Malcolm of Scotland, while many such as Gospatric fled north to join Edgar.

The king constructed and garrisoned a castle at York (now beneath Clifford's Tower) before returning south, throwing up further defences at Lincoln, Huntingdon and Cambridge en route. Then he paid off and disbanded his army.

In the aftermath of this campaign, William made Robert de Commines Earl of Northumbria. Robert reached Durham with a substantial following (reputedly of 500 or 900 men) but was there overwhelmed by local forces on 28 January 1069. This massacre signalled the start of the last great English rising against William. Robert fitzRichard from York was killed with his forces near the city and the leaders of Yorkshire combined with the far northerners and the exiles, who now rallied around Maerleswein and Edgar and besieged the castle. Their assault had not, however, succeeded when William arrived and routed them. He then constructed a second castle (the 'Old Baile'), placed William fitzOsbern in charge with large forces and returned to Winchester, all by Easter. FitzOsbern then defeated a second English attack and seems to have obtained control of the north.

That same summer brought two interventions from abroad. One was an attack by Harold's sons who raised parts of the south-west against the Normans. Their attack on Exeter and its new castle was, however, a failure, and local attacks on Robert of Mortain's castle at Montacute were defeated by the Bishop of Coutances with soldiers from London, Salisbury and Winchester.

More significant was the arrival of a great Danish fleet. Swein of Denmark had a far better claim to the English throne (by descent from Cnut) than had William and, with Norwegian competition at an end, he assembled a credible force for the invasion from Denmark and his Baltic neighbours. The Danish fleet arrived on the Narrows in late August but was repulsed at Dover, Sandwich and Ipswich before reaching the Humber in early September. There it was met by the northern rebels, grouped around Edgar, and by Earl Waltheof, who seems not to have broken with William until this point. At York, Archbishop Ealdred died at roughly the same time as the garrisons fired the town and, by accident, the minster, in preparation for the coming assault but they were themselves killed in the ensuing conflict. Elsewhere, the men of the core of Edwin's earldom took action against the Norman garrison at Shrewsbury.

William led an army north once more. According to one chronicler, he 'wholy ravaged and laid waste the shire', and it was on this occasion that the infamous wasting of Yorkshire and then Cheshire occurred, by which William destroyed the ability of the core territories of his opponents to sustain rebellion. The king kept court at mid-winter in the burnt-out wreck of York, then marched his army across the Pennines to suppress the Chester-centred Mercian rebellion, which he crushed in battle at Stafford.

The Danish fleet arguably represented the greatest threat to William's crown that he was to face in the early years of his reign. During the winter of 1069/70, it lay beyond his reach in the Humber, but the Danes seem to have been powerless to intervene in his destruction of the farms of their allies. By the time Swein himself arrived with reinforcements in 1070, the Northumbrians can have been in no condition to sustain his forces and they removed to the Fens where they plundered Peterborough before making peace with William and sailing for home.

The arrival of the initial Danish fleet provided English opponents of the Norman regime with the outside forces capable of giving resistance a real chance of success and their summary dispatch of the garrisons at York demonstrated their fighting qualities. This, however, proved to be the high point of Danish intervention. William out-manoeuvred and divided his opponents, so that he could severally defeat them or drive them off, and in the process the credibility of the Danes as an effective counterweight was undermined. There was to be no second Hastings-style conflict with the English crown as the prize.

In 1070 William returned south to Winchester to celebrate Easter. Although new Danish forces were at large, they no longer posed such a threat as they had done the previous autumn, and William's English enemies had been summarily defeated and their lands sequestered and plundered. A string of new castles, at Chester and Stafford for example, marked William's passage in arms, while his principal opponents had either fled or sought accommodation – and the latter group included Gospatric and Waltheof. At Winchester, William was accompanied by legates of Pope Alexander, who afterwards presided over a church synod at which Archbishop Stigand was formally deposed. Normans were promoted to the newly vacant see of York as well as Winchester, and Abbot Lanfranc of Caen to Canterbury.

The advancement of yet more incomers to English sees should be seen as part of what was now become a wholesale disestablishment of the native aristocracy and reallocation of their lands to Normans and other French followers of king William. This process did, of course, stimulate still more outbreaks of lawlessness and rebellion, as hitherto untouched estates became affected, but it is probably safe to concur with Brian Golding's judgement that the Winchester court at Easter 1070 represents the point in time when the Norman Conquest had become irreversible by force of arms alone.

EIGHT

A Troubled Kingship

William shattered internal opposition during the dramatic northern campaigns of 1069–70. Even so, his regime was still resented in some quarters and not everyone yet recognized the finality of his victory. Furthermore, he had already begun to experience the sort of problems that had earlier confronted Cnut: both could gather armies against a particular opponent but neither could solve the problems of governing, policing and defending disparate lordships separated by sea. Enemies within and without were encouraged by the very scale of William's territories to co-operate and attack him on several fronts.

William's opponents secured Maine in 1069 and then Flanders in 1071, where they killed his associate William fitzOsbern. News of this reverse may have encouraged opposition in England, where Edwin and Morcar fled the court. Edwin was murdered soon after but Morcar joined other dissidents and held Ely against the king. This last stand of the English nobility is popularly associated with Hereward the Wake, Abbot Brand's nephew, from whom Victorian sentimentalists fashioned a national hero, but it was as much a movement led by Morcar, the dispossessed Bishop Aethelwine of Durham and Siward Bearn, which looked once more to Danish reinforcement. With the exception of Hereward, all were captured by William.

Further north, the Scots remained hostile and had even raided Northumbria in 1070; Malcolm's connection with Edgar reinforced his importance. William led forces into Scotland in the autumn of 1073 and demanded Malcolm's surrender, but he did not secure Edgar's person. Nor did he entirely stop Malcolm assisting Edgar – indeed he fitted him out magnificently for an expedition to join Philip of France in 1074. However, William had more pressing concerns on the continent. The young Philip was constructing alliances with Flanders, Anjou and the Bretons against the overmighty duke, and these at times involved both Edgar and Malcolm. William countered by war: in 1073, he led an English and Norman army into Maine and regained control of the county. Yet even his

William's position was further weakened by growing competition for the succession among his three sons and their supporters, which led to the flight of Robert, the eldest, to Flanders and the company of his father's enemies. Robert had for some years been recognized as the ruler of Normandy in William's absence and his disaffection was serious. Among his supporters were other young men who were the sons of William's principal barons on both sides of the Channel. With French assistance, they defeated William at Gerberoi late in 1078 and forced the king to accept Robert's reinstatement as heir to his continental territories. Such setbacks weakened William's prestige and further encouraged his enemies to act against him.

Despite his worsening position on the continent, William's hold on England was surprisingly robust in the 1070s. Indicative of this was the ability of his lieutenants to put down the earls' rebellion. In this crisis the clergy were his principal supporters: Archbishop Lanfranc was in overall charge; Wulfstan, Bishop of Worcester, and Aethelwig, Abbot of Evesham, were prominent in preventing Earl Roger from advancing, while Bishops Odo and Geoffrey (of Coutances) outfaced Ralph, with the aid of castle garrisons, Norman soldiery and local levies. Once he had been crowned, loyalty to William was comparatively consistent throughout the senior English clergy, who were naturally disposed to be supportive of kingship and traditional hierarchies within the realm. As English bishops and abbots were gradually replaced by continental churchmen, loyalty to William became if anything more marked. Indeed, the priesthood were even vilified for their behaviour by Orderic:

> There were even some churchmen, wise and pious in
> outward appearance, who waited on the royal court out of
> covetousness for high office, and, to the great discredit of
> their cloth, shamelessly pandered to the king.

William made frequent demands on monasteries and bishops for armed men and this was arguably a factor in their subinfeudation of parts of their estates as knights' fees. Furthermore, he carried out some reorganization of England's dioceses, transferring several to new locations in or close to walled towns of his own choosing. The venerable see of Lichfield was, for example, transferred to Chester, where the bishop was expected to share in the oversight of the old capital of

Edwin's earldom. Dorchester-on-Thames was removed to Leicester, which was more central to the diocese and useful to William in controlling the south-east midlands. Yet such removals were not novel: the south-western dioceses had, for example, been reorganized under Edward and several sees had been refounded a century or more earlier following Viking raids.

Another feature of William's hold on England was the construction of castles. Indeed, this has often been seen as the most important factor, by which the 'new monarchy and the new feudalism were riveted on the land by the new military system', as Trevelyan remarked. There was certainly some novelty as regards these fortifications, most markedly in the building of massive mottes, and castles played an important role in suppressing rebellion in 1067–71. Castles provided secure accommodation for a new military élite, where men could sleep in safety and store their valuables and from which they could ride out to exercise control over the surrounding land, its surplus and its revenues. William clearly thought castle construction was the linchpin of his control of England, and it was so resented by the English that it was the first thing mentioned by the Peterborough monk in his bitter elegy of the king:

He had castles built and wretched men oppressed.

Yet castles were not quite as novel as they may appear. There has been some debate about their form in England, and some at least seem to have started as defended courtyards rather than motte-and-bailey types. If so, they were not unlike the defended halls of the late Anglo-Saxon aristocracy, examples of which have been excavated at Goltho and Sulgrave, the latter under a Norman ringwork. Even a thegn was expected to have a 'burh-gate', and many of the numerous local placenames in *burh* scattered across England testify to their prevalence. It is difficult to imagine that a great aristocratic stronghold such as Bamburgh was much different to a Norman castle. Yet castles were certainly important to the consolidation of Norman control and several contemporary accounts testify to the difficulties they posed to rebel forces.

As important to William's success was his tenure of the throne. In 1066 William took his place at the centre of a complex and comparatively effective system of government, which had a chancery and treasury. The demise of the great provincial aristocratic houses which had characterized late

Anglo-Saxon England enabled the first Norman king to take far more effective control of local government via the shire and hundredal courts and the office of sheriff. This was a welcome development for a king whose need to tax his subjects was far greater than his predecessor's. Despite his own vast landholdings, William used the geld system rigorously, to the point where few years passed without central taxes being raised. Domesday Book also reflects widespread increases in renders from both towns and countryside, which collectively suggest that landholders were exacting more from the remainder of society than hitherto, even while William and several of his barons were setting increasing amounts of land aside for hunting as royal forests or baronial chases. An important administrative innovation was the separation by William of church courts from those of the county. The Conqueror had greater freedom than his predecessors to introduce change on a national scale.

William used that freedom to transfer estates wholesale to a new aristocracy. In most instances, this process is obscure, with Domesday Book providing the earliest evidence. However, several features are clear. Some new landholdings were influenced by the structure of previous estates, with the king handing over to a single individual most of or even all of the lands held by one or a small group of precursors in a shire. So, for example, the Bishop of Lisieux's only estates in Buckinghamshire were those of Blackman, one of Tostig's followers, while William Peverel obtained all three of the manors held by Countess Gytha and seven of the numerous holdings of Alwin, a royal thegn. In other instances the king's desire to provide reliable oversight over strategically sensitive sites – and new castles – was critical, and this clearly affected the reconstruction of landholdings in Sussex. Some new honors were assembled without regard for earlier land-holding and constitute a real dislocation in the history of tenure and estate structure. In some peripheral areas William favoured the consolidation of estates into large honors, such as occurred at Richmond for Count Alan, but the principal beneficiaries in the long term were Earl Hugh at Chester and Earl Roger at Shrewsbury, to whom William effectively gave responsibility for the central and northern Welsh March, and control of entire shires.

In the west, William inherited the frontier problems which had beset his predecessors. Wales was less united, so less powerful, but more volatile since Gruffudd's death in 1063. FitzOsbern defeated three Welsh kings at Brecknock before his own death in 1071. Ceredigion in the far west was ravaged by 'the French' in the early 1070s and several Norman barons established themselves in Glamorganshire, constructing Cardiff castle, for example, around 1080. Baronies were created for the de Lacys, the Mortimers and the Cliffords, and each built castles. By 1086 Earl Roger had constructed castles at Shrewsbury and Hen Domen, near Montgomery, and the sheriff of Shropshire held Oswestry, while Hugh held Chester and his kinsman had built Rhuddlan. Both gave lands along the frontier to bellicose followers and then advanced to acquire control of fresh Welsh territory, building castles and establishing military colonies. Roger pushed into southern Powys while Hugh advanced along the northern coasts and invaded Gwynedd itself, where he was confronted from 1075 by Gruffudd's son, following Bleddyn's death in civil war. In such circumstances the Welsh princes were incapable of opposing William's claims to oversight of Wales and were hard-pressed to retain control even of the far west, particularly when the king himself invaded in 1081.

In the north William reinforced his Norman archbishop by giving authority beyond Yorkshire to Bishop Walcher, a Lotharingian whom he appointed to Durham in 1076. Walcher's position presages the creation of the county palatinate, but he was killed by the Northumbrians in 1080. William responded with punitive expeditions, the second of which, led by his son Robert, renewed peace with Malcolm and built the 'Newcastle' on the Tyne. The formidable William de St Calais was established at Durham and further Norman appointments were made to the earldom, and their positions were rendered tenable by enfeoffing Count Alan, Ilbert de Lacy and Drogo with castleries at Richmond, Pontefract and Holderness respectively. To the west, Roger of Poitou was established at Penwortham and granted the bulk of what was to become Lancashire, but the Norman occupation of Cumbria would be delayed until William Rufus secured Carlisle from the Scots in 1092. The task of reconstruction after the traumatic events of 1069–70 was to take a generation and would result in many changes in the north, both as regards the geography of power and the organization and settlement of the very landscape itself.

NINE

William, Domesday and the Danes: 1085–7

Domesday Book is the best known document of the Middle Ages and is often accounted William's finest achievement. It is also among the more enigmatic: the Domesday Inquest was established at midwinter 1085/6, and the list of questions has survived in the *Ely Inquest*, but the final digest – Great Domesday Book – was apparently abandoned, incomplete, before William's departure for France late in 1086. None recorded its purpose before Richard fitzNigel, Henry II's long-serving treasurer late in the twelfth century, who remarked that it ensured that every 'man should know his right and not usurp another's', claiming the authority of Bishop Henry, William's long-dead grandson.

Modern opinion of William's purpose is divided. In 1909 Round argued that it was a geld book but this was discredited by Galbraith in the 1960s, who viewed it instead as a 'formal written record of the introduction of feudal tenure'. Since Galbraith, historians have argued that the survey addressed a variety of objectives, albeit that each has preferred a slightly different set. Sally Harvey, for example, argued that William's purpose was geld reform. Following James Holt, all are, however, now inclined to look to the immediate political circumstances of the survey for an explanation.

In 1085 the English believed that an attack from Denmark was imminent, launched by King Cnut Sweinsson in alliance with Flanders. Danish fleets had repeatedly posed the biggest external threat to William, with major incursions in 1069, 1070 and 1075. Cnut had experience of command. The Flemish connection suggests a link too with others of William's opponents, such as Philip of France, and implies that William's French opponents hoped to co-ordinate attacks on Normandy with a Viking descent on England: Fulk of Anjou had again attacked Maine in 1081 and overrun Brittany.

William could expect no external aid and his regime was weakened by losses (Queen Matilda died in 1083) and disaffections within the family (Odo was imprisoned in 1082 and Robert was in revolt).

He had already ordered an exceptional geld of 6s on the hide in 1083–4, perhaps collected over three years, and was in Normandy in 1085, confronting his enemies. He crossed to England at the news with 'a larger force of mounted men and infantry . . . than had ever come to this country'. The provisioning of these mercenaries was achieved by dispersing them among his vassals, who 'fed the army, each in proportion to his land', and William additionally ordered the coastal lands to be wasted to deny supplies to the Danes.

On top of the geld of 1083–4, wasting had a serious impact on specific regions and billeting imposed heavy burdens. Allocation of troops was arguably based on geld lists, and it should be recalled that royal and some comital and church estates were unhidated and so geld-exempt. The weight of billeting fell, therefore, disproportionately on the lesser tenants-in-chief and rear vassals.

When the Danes failed to arrive, William paid off some mercenaries but retained others, presumably anticipating attack in 1086. Funds were raised but a contemporary remarked that 'the land is already harassed by many misfortunes through the collection of royal money'. The prestige of the regime was low, with William committed to fighting a defensive and expensive war of indeterminate length against a distant enemy. By Christmas 1085 many of those worst hit by the government's measures had reason to be disaffected.

The king and his vassals spent Christmas at Gloucester and he presided over a church synod there. Then William 'had much thought and deep discussion with his council about this country – how it was occupied or with what sort of people' and initiated the Domesday Inquest. In considering this decision, it is important to stress that William's regime was not acting at leisure or from a position of over-riding majesty but in the context of military crisis, internal distress and financial need.

On 1 August that year William met his vassals and, significantly, *their* vassals, at Salisbury, and received new oaths of allegiance. This implies that the allegiance of the Norman establishment in England had been suspect over the winter but that William had found the means to reaffirm their commitment to his regime. With renewed confidence in the English political situation, William then returned to Normandy. How had the situation changed?

One factor must certainly be the assassination of

Cnut IV at Odensee in July 1086, on the eve of departure. Cnut's death not only removed the immediate threat of invasion but actually brought to an end Scandinavian attacks on western Europe – and so in a sense marks the ending of the Viking Age. Although this broader meaning was not apparent in 1086, it did enable William to ship his troops over to Normandy to confront his French opponents. Cnut's death did not, however, impact upon the great oath-swearing ceremony at Salisbury, since that was necessarily arranged before news from Denmark reached England. Indeed, it was probably established at the Christmas council, along with the Domesday Inquest. It would seem, therefore, that it was the making of Domesday Book which was the *quid pro quo* that persuaded the aristocracy to recommit themselves to William in the high summer.

What did Domesday Book offer the Norman aristocracy? One valuable aspect was confirmation of tenure. The transfer of lands from Anglo-Saxon to Norman landholders had necessarily been a messy and *ad hoc* affair, leading to numerous conflicts between claimants. Some lands were held illegally and numerous claims were recorded – but few settled – in the folios of Domesday Book, although the majority of manors could be assigned to a particular tenant and tenant-in-chief. Domesday Book certainly was later used to defend title to land – as William fitzNigel recorded – and William's vassals are likely to have seen the advantages to themselves. It is difficult, however, to see this as a sufficiently pressing need to bring the Domesday Inquest into existence in the difficult days of midwinter, 1085/6.

Besides its value as a work of reference for the settlement of claims, Holt suggested two other purposes for Domesday Book, namely the centralization of information concerning the king's lands and as a reference work for the purposes of collecting feudal dues, such as escheats and wardship. Both were obviously important, but primarily to the royal regime. Although it might be argued that a regularization of feudal dues might benefit the baronage (particularly since William charged high entry fines to heirs to retain family estates), this cannot have been crucial to the resolution of the king's difficulties in 1086.

If Domesday *was* a concession to the middle-range of Norman and English landholders, then it was arguably designed to head off their current grievances. It was not directed at geld, so it arguably had some utility as regards the billeting of William's great army of 1085, some of which he still retained at Christmas and more of which he was presumably planning to hire in the summer. Since neither William nor his Anglo-Saxon predecessors had previously faced the problems inherent in billeting large numbers of mercenaries, Domesday Book looks like a new solution to a novel problem.

In 1085 the problem centred on use of the Anglo-Saxon geld system as a basis on which to apportion billeting. Hides (and, in the Danelaw, carucates) were the basis of land tax and it presumably made sense that royal estates and those of some favoured landholders did not contribute, since a king does not pay tax to himself on his own rents and produce. Many great men had organized their holdings so that a disproportionate amount of the gross geld liability of their estates was paid by their tenants rather than themselves. That these unhidated and beneficially hidated manors should be exempt from billeting was another matter, and this was where Domesday Book made a critical contribution. It created a register of all estates, both hidated and unhidated, organized so as to make it possible to allocate the burden of billeting far more fairly than previously.

Domesday Book was a centrally held record of the resources of each shire, manor by manor, grouped by tenancies-in-chief. Individual entries normally included the following information: the manor name, current tenant, geld liability, number of ploughlands and working ploughs and their distribution within the manor, both in lordship and among tenancies of varying status, other assets (including mills, churches, meadow and woodland), the landholder in 1066 and his/her status, and the value, both current and 'in the time of King Edward'.

Clearly, some information was edited out of the initial compilation – Little Domesday Book, which covers East Anglia, includes numbers of livestock, for example, but this does amount to valuable information for the purpose of replacing the geld as a basis for the billeting of troops.

In particular, two categories of data may have been intended as a short-cut to the fairer allocation of billeting: ploughlands and manorial valuations. Supposing ploughlands were literally a measure of agricultural land – and that is contentious – then

97

that could provide a rough guide to the production capacity of an estate, but there were clearly difficulties in practice in collecting this information. Valuations may therefore have been intended for this purpose, and it is noticeable that they frequently occupy the last line of an entry, sign-posted effectively by the enlarged capital letter with which the next begins. Valuations do in a sense provide an arithmetic summation of the individual manor, which royal officials at the centre and in the shire may well have intended to use to assign mercenaries to particular honors.

The Domesday Inquest was conducted in great haste and in an atmosphere of crisis. It necessarily had the enthusiastic support of the aristocracy, who helped to collect the data, and who presumably anticipated benefits to themselves. The process culminated in a great oath-taking, by which William renewed his hold on the baronage in England.

With this achieved and Cnut dead, William was free to raise fresh revenues and return to France late in 1086, where he was on the diplomatic offensive once more, marrying his daughter Constance to Alan IV of Brittany.

In 1087 William struck at King Philip's tenure of

the Vexin and in an exceptionally brutal campaign destroyed Mantes, but was taken ill there and retired to Rouen, and eventually to the priory of St Gervais. There, on his deathbed, he consulted his younger sons and other courtiers and named his successors. Normandy went to Robert, as promised, but he nominated William Rufus to England, in a manner which recalls the division of many cross-Channel Norman baronies over the previous decade and more. Neither Rufus nor Henry, the youngest son, stayed to witness their father's death on 9 September, after which his corpse was abandoned by the great and despoiled by his lesser attendants, who took 'the arms, the plate, the linen and the royal furniture'.

William was eventually interred in the monastery of St Stephen which he had built in Caen, but the ceremony was disrupted by a fire in the city, claims made against his appropriation of the land on which the church had been built and finally by difficulties in forcing his massive corpse into the stone coffin prepared for it. So perished the Conqueror.

TEN

The Conquest in Retrospect

The Norman Conquest was controversial even within William's own lifetime, and this comes over very clearly in differing summations of his achievements at his death. A monk at Caen, a house which William had himself founded, wrote: 'This king excelled in wisdom all the princes of his generation, and among them he was outstanding in the largeness of his soul.' This is clearly sycophancy, but writers other than William's apologists paid tribute to his qualities. Orderic Vitalis remarked that:

> The king's passion for justice dominated the kingdom,
> encouraging others to follow his example. He struggled to
> learn some of the English language, so that he could
> understand the pleas of the conquered people without an
> interpreter, and benevolently pronounce fair judgements for
> each one as justice required. But advancing age prevented
> him,

100

England and took service at Byzantium to escape William's kingship, and such might have agreed with the sentiments expressed by Francis Palgrave in 1837 that 'the spot where Harold's standard had been cast down was the grave of the pride and glory of England'. Sir Frank Stenton identified only two Englishmen holding substantial estates in 1086, Thorkell of Warwick (132 hides) and Colswein of Lincoln (100 carucates). Research primarily by Ann Williams has added a few others such as Edward of Salisbury and Gospatric, son of Arnkell. Two categories of survivors emerge: men with family links with King Edward (such as Harold, Earl Ralph's heir) whom William arguably acknowledged as his own relatives, and some of Edward's officials whose service to the new king preserved their estates through the early and most dangerous years. To these Chris Lewis has suggested that Edward's Norman and French courtiers should be added, but even with all possible additions pre-Conquest holders and their heirs form only a tiny proportion of the aristocracy in 1086. William's appointments to high office in the church were consistently in favour of immigrants, and English priests and monks had cause for resentment at the obstruction of their own advancement under King William. He certainly presided over a transfer of land and lordship which dwarfed anything attempted by Cnut a half century earlier, even if that had not been his initial intention.

In some senses, William's land-holding revolution also amounted to a wider shift in terms of status and land-tenure. Anglo-Saxon estates were subject to a variety of public obligations (such as the geld and military service) and many derived from royal grants, as surviving charters make clear. Some were consequent upon public office, and this is particularly true of the earls, who were the king's principal lieutenants. There was not, however, a feudal theory under which all land was held of the crown, since family lands were inherited. William's grants necessarily changed this, since there was little left in England of inherited land and the élite held fiefs or honors of the king. Yet it is difficult to demonstrate clear differences in the flow of obligations as a consequence of conquest. The new Norman landholders expected to hold their new estates with all the rights and obligations of Anglo-Saxon thegns. The old view of a feudal revolution under the Normans is now waning and it is probably appropriate that it should.

There were, however, some real changes. In the dangerous years immediately following 1066, William imposed quotas of knights on English fiefs and these were eventually set at specific numbers of knights' fees. Rather than maintain household knights in sufficient numbers, bishops and monasteries enfeoffed men with parts of their estates in return for a part of their contracted military obligations, and over the years these rear-vassals were successful in demanding heritable tenure, and so in turn obtained the rights of the Old English thegnage. It was this mêlée of substantial honors and individual holdings, separated by entire layers of subinfeudation from the crown, that constituted the most significant shift in land-tenure in the early Norman period. Even so, there was no clear demarcation between such knights' fees at the lower end and free tenure in socage, which descended from Anglo-Saxon landholding. It may well be that numerous cross-ethnic marriages occurred at this level, such as spawned Orderic Vitalis for example, with a consequent mixing of English and Norman families and styles of land-tenure. Additionally, it is unclear to what extent subinfeudation and ministerial tenancies existed in

Anglo-Saxon England. It may well be that the oft-quoted contrast is more a matter of different types of evidence than substantial differences in tenure, particularly in areas from which royal influence was largely excluded before 1066.

A less contentious change was the demolition of the great earldoms of late Anglo-Saxon England. Perhaps two hundred individuals were the principal beneficiaries of William's reallocation of lands, but none held the sort of power or concentrations of land that had been the hallmark of Godwine's or Leofric's families. The title of earl was retained by William but used more freely and normally in relation to single shires. With specific exceptions on the periphery of England, it became primarily honorific rather than functional. Indeed, the rebellion of the earls in the 1070s may have owed something to conflicting views on what an earldom conferred. Shire-reeves had been significant in the interaction of the centre and the shires before the Conquest, but William gave unfettered power to the office, which probably accounts for complaints concerning the venality of many early Norman sheriffs. That is not to say that the greater Norman lords lacked power or resources. For example, their collective pressure on Wales was particularly telling in the years following William's death, when they killed Rhys ap Tewdwr and established castles in the far west. But the monolithic territorial earldoms of Edward's reign had gone and the estates of William's earls were more widely scattered across England and interspersed with others than those of their predecessors.

Beneath the great lordships, it is difficult to judge the impact of Norman rule in the countryside. There are some apparent differences between descriptions of status in late Anglo-Saxon England and the Norman period, with, for example, the rapid disappearance of slavery, but this may be no more than a matter of terminology. Anglo-Saxon demesne slaves were arguably the ploughmen of Norman lordships. The peasantry probably paid higher levels of rent and labour dues after the Conquest, and lost whatever shreds of free status some of them still retained, but population growth and land-hunger were arguably the principal drivers, rather than Norman tyranny. Again, there seems to have been widespread nucleation of villages during the Norman period and on into the early years of the thirteenth century, associated with the adoption of open field agriculture, but this was already in process before the Conquest and was arguably determined more by long-term opportunities than short-term pressures. Norman kings and lords perhaps had a greater responsibility for the foundation or validation of new boroughs, but growth in the cash economy was the essential prerequisite of greater economic specialization and Anglo-Saxon kings had a healthy reputation as regards town-foundation.

Norman lordship has been more successful than Anglo-Saxon in leaving memorials to itself. Contemporaries in England and Wales were agreed that castles were important to the Norman tenure of disputed territory. Indeed, annals regularly focus on their significance. Take, for example, an extract from the Welsh *Kings of the Saxons* for 1093:

> And two months after that, about the Calends of July, the French overran Dyfed and Ceredigion; and they have ruled them from that day to this. And they controlled all Wales and built castles in it and fortified others.

Whether or not castles would have become an established part of the British Middle Ages without the Normans must remain in doubt, but their ruins necessarily bear testimony to the Conquest and its aftermath. Less noticeable but as commonplace are the remains of Norman churches. In general, Anglo-Saxon churches were small and their architecture did not satisfy the pretensions of the incoming French and Norman clerics, who pulled many down and built anew. In some instances, as at Canterbury and York, reconstruction was necessitated by accidental destruction but in many others it was a matter of choice. The process produced some of the finest cathedral architecture in Europe, at Durham for example, alongside a plethora of small, local churches. If limited to naming just one, historians would certainly opt for different examples, but it is difficult to find another small Anglo-Norman church as interesting as that at Kilpeck, Herefordshire. Elsewhere, the late eleventh and twelfth centuries witnessed a massive investment in the renewal of pre-existing Anglo-Saxon monasteries, the refoundation of examples which had long since foundered – particularly in the north – and investment in entirely new houses, which were increasingly established by new religious orders, such as the Cistercians and Augustinians, during the twelfth century.

Just as Cnut's reign reinforced connections

between Denmark and England, so did William's between England and north-west France. This can be seen in aspects such as trade, but it also emerges in cultural borrowings. The English language survived the Normans comparatively unaltered, but it certainly lost status as a language of literature, record and government. The Norman impact on place-naming is minor, with examples generally limited to new sites, such as castles, or the addition of a suffix to distinguish similar settlement names, as at Crosby Garrett (Gerard), Cumbria. It is in the area of personal naming that English suffered its most drastic setback. By the second half of the twelfth century, very few infants were being given English names, Edward excepted. Rather, it was becoming commonplace for even villagers to name their children William or Roger or Hugh – Norman names. English women's names retreated less rapidly and perhaps less far. This may have been because more English women survived in positions where they were capable of influencing fashion, but it may have been because female names were less critical to the status and security of the family and its landholdings.

A significant factor differentiating Danish from Norman influence on England must be the timescale. William's reign was barely longer than that of Cnut. Had the separation of his lands on his deathbed proved permanent, the Norman impact on England might rapidly have dissipated and the whole affair been relegated to the status of a footnote in history. However, William Rufus and then Henry I engineered their elder brother's downfall and the reconstitution of William's lordships so that Norman cultural influences were reinforced and cross-Channel landholding reinvigorated over a lengthy second generation. The long period of warfare between Henry's daughter (Matilda) and his nephew (Stephen) was finally resolved in 1154 with the succession of Henry II, Matilda's son, whose lordships included England and all western France, from Anjou to the Atlantic. Not until John lost his northern French territories to the French crown in the early years of the thirteenth century was this umbilical cord to perish and even thereafter the kings of England retained the Duchy of Guienne and pretensions to wider French territories.

Later events were to strengthen greatly the Normanization of England, therefore, but it would be a mistake to imagine that such had been William the Bastard's intention when he undertook his grandest and most risky of enterprises in 1066. Then – in Norman accounts – God gave him victory on account of Harold's broken oaths. In the opinion of the conquered, it was a punishment of the sins of the English, from which they ultimately expected deliverance. It was their perception of events that was revived by patriotic Victorians, such as Edward Freeman in 1869, to whose partiality we might perhaps permit the last word:

> After the errors and follies of his reign, Eadward died, not purely a saint, but as an Englishman and a patriot. . . .
> England was to have an English King, the noblest man of the English people.

His description of the battle of Hastings was to be mercilessly contested by J.H. Round, but he claimed the authority of late eleventh- and twelfth-century commentators for his summation:

> In the eyes of men of the next generation that day was the fatal day of England, the day of the sad overthrow of our dear country, the day of her handing over to foreign lords.

111

Further Reading

PRIMARY SOURCES IN TRANSLATION

There are three major collections of sources for this period: Whitelock, D. (ed.), *English Historical Documents* (London, Eyre and Spottiswoode, vol. I, 500–1042, 2nd edn 1979, reissued by Routledge, 1996); Douglas, D. and Greenaway, G.W. (eds), *English Historical Documents* (London, Eyre and Spottiswoode, vol. II, 1042–1189, 2nd edn 1981, reissued Routledge, 1996); and Allen Brown, R. (ed.), *The Norman Conquest: Documents of Medieval History 5* (London, Edward Arnold, 1984).

The *Anglo-Saxon Chronicle* is available in several translations, the best and most recent, which is generally used herein, being Swanton, M. (trans. and ed.), *The Anglo-Saxon Chronicle* (London, Dent, 1996). Other quotations from early sources are taken from: Barlow, F. (trans. and ed.), *The Life of King Edward the Confessor* (London, Thomas Nelson & Sons, 1962); Bosanquet, G. (trans.), *Eadmer's History of Recent Events in England* (London, Cresset Press, 1964); Chibnall, M. (ed.), *The Ecclesiastical History of Orderic Vitalis* (Oxford, Clarendon Press, 6 vols, 1969–80); Jones, T. (trans. and ed.), *Brut Y Tywysogyon* or *The Chronicle of the Princes* (Cardiff, University of Wales Press, 2nd edn 1973). *Domesday Book* is most easily accessible via the county volumes in Morris, J. (ed.), *History from the Sources* (Chichester, Phillimore).

SECONDARY LITERATURE

Barlow, F., *Edward the Confessor* (London, Eyre and Spottiswoode, 1970), is the standard bibliography of the last Anglo-Saxon king, and the same author developed his views on the impact of the Conquest in *The Feudal Kingdom of England* (Harlow, Longman, 1980). For the views of the other great doyen of Norman studies of the last generation, see Allen Brown, R., *The Norman Conquest* (London, Edward Arnold, 1984), but Loyn, H.R., *Anglo-Saxon England and the Norman Conquest* (Harlow, Longman, 2nd edn 1991), has many useful insights, as have the comments of Eric John in Campbell, J. (ed.), *The Anglo-Saxons* (London, Phaidon, 1982).

Chibnall, M., *The World of Orderic Vitalis* (Oxford, Clarendon Press, 1984), places the important writings of Orderic in their political, social and cultural context.

Clanchy, M.T., *England and its Rulers, 1066–1272* (Oxford, Blackwell, 2nd edn 1998), provides an invigorating overview which harnesses contemporary opinion very effectively.

Clarke, P.A., *The English Nobility under Edward the Confessor* (Oxford, Clarendon Press, 1994), attempts to reconstruct the late Anglo-Saxon aristocracy.

Douglas, D.C., *William the Conqueror: the Norman impact upon England* (Berkeley and Los Angeles, 1964), was the key advocate of his generation of William's personal greatness.

Fleming, R., *Kings and Lords in Conquest England* (Cambridge, Cambridge University Press, 1991), reviews land-tenure across the Conquest and particularly in Edward's reign, with reference to the great earldoms.

FURTHER READING

Freeman, E.A., *The History of the Norman Conquest* (Oxford, Clarendon Press, 3 vols, 1869), is the heavyweight pro-English vision of 1066 as an undiluted national tragedy.

Golding, B., *Conquest and colonisation: the Normans in Britain, 1066–1100* (London, Macmillan, 1994), offers a balanced review of the history of early Norman England.

Grape, W., *The Bayeux Tapestry* (Munich & New York, Prestel, 1994), offers controversial new ideas about the Bayeux Tapestry.

Higham, N.J., *The Death of Anglo-Saxon England* (Stroud, Sutton, 1997), reviews the royal succession and its political context over the last century of Anglo-Saxon England, including 1066.

Hill, D. (ed.), *Ethelred the Unready: papers from the millenniary conference*, British Archaeological Reports, Oxford, 1978, remains a seminal collection and the same author's *An Atlas of Anglo-Saxon England* (Oxford, Blackwell, 1981) is by far the best atlas of the period.

John, E., *Reassessing Anglo-Saxon England* (Manchester, University Press, 1996), offers the most trenchant recent defence of William's candidacy as Edward the Confessor's own preference.

Kapelle, W.E., *The Norman Conquest of the North: the region and its transformation, 1000–1135* (London, Croom Helm, 1979), remains the best study of the Normans in Northumbria.

Keynes, S., *The Diplomas of King Aethelred 'The Unready', 978–1016* (Cambridge, University Press, 1980), is a seminal study of Aethelred's reign and his several regimes.

114

Lawson, M.K., *Cnut: the Danes in England in the early eleventh century* (London, Longman, 1993), is the only monograph on the history of Cnut's reign currently in print.

Lewis, C.P., 'The French in England before the Norman Conquest', in *Anglo-Norman Studies*, 17 (1994), 123–44, reviews Edward's Norman and French friends and their lands.

Morillo, S., *The Battle of Hastings: Sources and Interpretations* (Woodbridge, Boydell Press, 1996), contains a wealth of discussion about 1066 and the various strands of William's campaigns on land and sea.

Palgrave, P., *History of the Anglo-Saxons* (London, John Murray, 1837), was an early portrayal of the Conquest as a national tragedy.

Round, J.H., *Feudal England* (London, Swan Sonnenshein & Co., 1909), rejected the patriotic, anti-Norman sentiments that fuelled so many nineteenth-century histories, and particularly attacked Freeman's vision of the period.

Rumble, A. (ed.), *The Reign of Cnut: King of England, Denmark and Norway* (Leicester, University Press, 1994), contains essays on many aspects of Cnut's reign.

Sawyer, P.H., *Kings and Vikings, Scandinavia and Europe: AD 700–1100* (London, Methuen, 1982), remains an invigorating and challenging study of the period which famously minimizes the numbers of Vikings involved in raids on western Europe.

Stafford, P., *Unification and Conquest: a political and social history of England in the tenth and eleventh centuries* (London, Edward

Arnold, 1989), provides the best overview of the creation of the single kingship of Anglo-Saxon England.

Stenton, F.M., *Anglo-Saxon England* (Oxford, University Press, 3rd edn, 1971), remains a classic study of early England, but see, too, his much earlier *William the Conqueror* (London, Frank Cass, 1908).

Strickland, M. (ed.), *Anglo-Norman Warfare* (Woodbridge, Boydell, 1992), deals exclusively with war and offers useful insights into military organization in eleventh-century England and Normandy.

Williams, A., *The English and the Norman Conquest* (Woodbridge, Boydell Press, 1995), is in many ways the most interesting current study of the Conquest, concentrating as it does on the role of the English in early Norman England.

Index